elements

elements

architecture in detail

edited by oscar riera ojeda

introduction by mark pasnik

chapter headings and captions by james mccown

photography by paul warchol

First published in the United States of America by Rockport Publishers, Inc.
33 Commercial Street
Gloucester, Massachusetts 01930-5089
Telephone: (978) 282-9590
Fax: (978) 283-2742
www.rockpub.com

Library of Congress Cataloging-in-Publication data available.

design by oscar riera ojeda and lucas guerra

layout by oscar riera ojeda

ISBN 1-56496-931-2

10 9 8 7 6 5 4 3 2 1

Manufactured in China by Palace Press International.

Cover photograph: Steven Holl Architects, Museum of Contemporary Art, Helsinki, Finland, 1998. Previous page: Shelton, Mindel & Associates, Manhattan Rooftop Residence, New York, 1997. This spread: Gluckman Mayner Architects, Helmut Lang SoHo, New York, 1998. Contents page: François de Menil, Architect, Bank Street Residence, Houston, 2000.

Back flap photography credits: portraits of Mark Pasnik and Oscar Riera Ojeda © Lisa Pascarelli (top) and Paul Warchol © Abraham Aronow (bottom).

rockport publishers

contents

introduction by mark pasnik

Imagine a detail from one of the iconic works of twentieth century architecture: Louis Kahn's Exeter Library. The railing at the top of the grand stair doubles as a seat. Its form matches that of the stair's handrail, but its panel morphs into a continuous profile reflecting the human contour. This element is fashioned entirely from travertine, making no differentiation between the seatback and the banister [figure 1]; its form is simply an indivisible extrusion. Such material uniformity belies a functioning duality.

■ It was the compelling nature of this kind of duality that emerged as Oscar Riera Ojeda and I developed this book. When we initially conceived the *Architecture in Detail* series, our thematic interests centered on the detailed expression of architectural elements. Rooted in historical definitions of the term, we had perceived elements to be quantifiable and irreducible architectural forms, basic indivisible units, singular and unique pieces, functionally pure and recognizable parts of a building. This book, then, began as an attempt to produce a catalogue of various elements that would represent the way in which architects are practicing at the small scale today. Although from the outset we were aware of the impossibility of creating a comprehensive resource in a single book, we shared a naïve optimism that we could provide a general index of element types—doors, windows, walls, columns, stairs, railings, and so on—while representing the diversity and complexity of contemporary practice in a range of innovative forms. ■ Yet as we scoured the thousands of images in photographer Paul Warchol's archive—images taken

core vocabulary of the classical language. Vitruvius, for example, classified temple archetypes and described the three orders from which they are composed. He perceived the orders as "elementary forms" to be arranged according to specific customs and in a fashion in which "the separate parts and the whole design may harmonize in their proportions and symmetry."[1] Fundamentally, his writings emphasize the fixed and predetermined codification of elements as they relate to one another in definitions of classicism.

■ A millennium and a half later, Palladio began his four-part treatise with a book nearly dedicated to describing the components that comprise a building, from its foundation and walls, its columns (and this time the expanded five ancient orders), rooms, pavements and ceilings, vaults, doors and windows, chimneys, staircases [figure 10], and ending with roofs. The text follows the sequence in which a building might be physically assembled. In doing so, Palladio underscores the relationship of each element to the larger structure, where "every part or member stands in its due place...." He continues: "Beauty will result from the form and correspondence of the whole, with respect to the several parts, of the parts with regard to each other, and of these again to the whole...."[2] As with Vitruvius, the emphasis here is on the "agreement" of parts according to regulations and conventions, a condition in which it was necessary to relegate elements to the status of pure and predetermined components.

■ The premises of this tradition have long held firm in definitions of the element. Even today, in a variety of practices, we see the

consuming hybrids

over the past three decades—we quickly noted that many of the contemporary elements we admired most would simply not fit comfortably into neat categories. We discovered among the images that a stair might double as a light shaft, a wall and floor might be continuous and inseparable, in general that elements today are less likely to be pure, irreducible, or even identifiable. As attractive as the idea of a catalogue was for us, it became all too apparent that this book would more accurately portray today's preoccupations in architectural practice by emphasizing those elements that *deny* the very structure of the catalogue we had set out to create. ■ Somehow, we still could not ignore the pressures of history. The very idea of the element as a foundational and irreducible architectural component has evolved from the history of publications on the principles of architectural expression, first in written treatises, later in illustrated ones. The most widely influential of these—*The Ten Books on Architecture* by Vitruvius and *The Four Books of Architecture* by Andrea Palladio—are catalogues of the elements that form the

remnants of the classical understanding of elements, evoked to even stricter codification. Perhaps the most vivid illustrations of this condition are in two disparate ideological camps of the profession. On the one hand, elements are treated as repeatable forms in the global modern vocabularies of corporate firms, where identical details are carried from project to project to project. On the other hand, New Urbanists promote stringent and prescriptive guidelines in which architectural codes are advanced to the level of legally binding zoning ordinances and developmental guidelines. An even more widespread American phenomenon is the industry-wide dependence on resources such as Sweet's Catalog and the Home Depot, leading to a crass standardization of details. ■ At their most extreme, these positions promote strategies for practice in which the whole is extrapolated from a fixed language of elements by combining them in new ways. This kit of parts ultimately limits the potential for invention to that of the relationships among predetermined elements, while stifling the possibility of rethinking the ways in which elements behave or the nature of the elements themselves. Such an approach recalls a department store chain's television jingle: "The right choices…make all the difference." The message: so long as you have a good selection, you'll make good choices. ■ But is this enough? ■ Above all, we hope this book will be a provocative and challenging springboard to thinking creatively about elements. So where the eighteenth-century French essayist Marc-Antoine Laugier described the classical tradition as a search for "fixed and unchangeable laws,"[3] we have aimed to investigate a very different ideology present in today's work, specifically a tendency within contemporary thinking to explore the conflicts, inconsistencies, and tensions that exist within architectural culture. We have thus assembled elements that often contradict the associations of purity or indivisibility traditionally ascribed to typological forms. In these cases, the elements are often defined in grayer terms. ■ In addressing this philosophical shift in the element, is it important to recognize the modern movement's involvement. As various strains of modernism developed in the early twentieth century, elements remained at the expressive center of what Le Corbusier termed "a new epoch" and its search for new forms. Yet the emergence of new modernist sensibilities recast the definition of elements as malleable pieces of the part-to-whole equation. New conceptions of space and representation appeared early on, visualized in the Cubist still-life paintings of Braque or Picasso, in which the objects represented were described through the expression of

the frame between wall and door panel, forming an element with conjoined attributes. The wall is an extension of the door and the door is continuous with the surface of the wall. Yet the door has none of the characteristics of a secret panel, because it was never meant to disguise itself as something other than what it is (the treatment of the floor panel below it precludes any misconceptions). This modernist vision creates an architectural equivalent to the mythical Minotaur's crossing of human and animal form: elements come together to form a new whole, but one in which the origins—the parts—are still visible. They are unified amalgamations, even if their identifies are not yet entirely seamless. ■ What is unique about details in the last decade's resurgent modern movement is a shift from elements that are conjoined to those that are hybrids. The hybrid yet again fuses several elements, but jettisons the identity of component pieces in favor of the inseparability—both conceptual and visual—of the larger whole. Tension and conflicts remain in the visual relationships of the functional elements, which are evidenced in the whole, but now seamlessly intertwined. They form an Escher-like illusion of mysterious overlaps, confusions of pieces, and the blurred layering that is far more complex than classicism's basic type-forms and relationships of parts to whole. Thus, the very definition of elements is loosened in a manner that enriches the creative potential for architects to make new forms, to propose and express new ideas about program, and ultimately to invent new intersections in the way people occupy and use spaces. ■ In part because

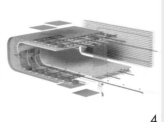

multiple vantage points simultaneously. Such developments enabled architects to change the way in which elements operated. With the maturing of modernism, it became possible to create elements composed of an amalgamation of parts—a sheet of glass that doubled as a door, or a roof that was also a garden. In such instances, functionally pure elements could be assembled into simultaneous compositions that form a larger conjoined unit. ■ Given their well-known preoccupation with details, it is perhaps no surprise that we see such explorations in the architecture of Louis Kahn and Carlo Scarpa. Revealing his own preoccupations, Kahn admired Scarpa's "sense of the wholeness of inseparable parts."[4] In contrast to classical systems, here the parts themselves have become grounds for creative exploration. In a manner similar to Kahn's aforementioned bench-handrail at Exeter, Carlo Scarpa's Palazzo Querini Stampalia in Venice includes a door leading from the main exhibition hall to a side chamber [figure 2]. The door is nothing more than a pivoting travertine panel set within the larger stone panels of the wall. Scarpa has eliminated

of the types of experimentation enabled by advances in computer modeling, we see this redefinition of elements most clearly in the unbuilt experimental projects of today's avant-garde practices. As examples, I wish to mention two recent projects described in computer renderings, both of which give conceptual prominence to an often-uncelebrated element of a building—its core. ■ The first is a proposal by Elizabeth Diller and Ricardo Scofidio. As designers who are known for art and architecture projects that fuse often opposed media, Diller + Scofidio employ similar tactics of fusion in their competition-winning entry for the Eyebeam Building in New York [figures 3–4]. The entire building is formed from a continuous, two-ply ribbon, which dissolves walls and floors into an unbroken undulating surface containing the building's support systems between its two layers. Functionally this is little more than a cleverly planned chase for wires. Yet conceptually, the core is reconfigured as an element that expresses the interaction of art and media, while creating spaces that encourage the producers (students, artists, and staff) to intermingle with the observers (museum visitors and theater-goers). In doing so, the architects have underscored the element's capacity to assert social and programmatic effects in architecture. ■ The second example is at a smaller scale. In his Torus House, Preston Scott Cohen has devised an equally complex element that serves as a building core [figure 5]. Obeying convention, this core is positioned at the center of the house, partitioning the mid-level living spaces and connecting a lower-level carport to a roof terrace. Yet it contains unconventionally indeterminate functional attributes: is it a staircase, a courtyard, a light well, an impluvium—or all of these things? This sophisticated layering of simultaneous functions adds complexity to our first reading of the core as a singular piece. And while we still may see it as an identifiable object within the space, it merges at its seams with the ceiling and floor, becoming a part of the larger continuity of surface around it. Contradictions indeed: an object that is not; a connector, centerpiece, and divider; an indeterminate purpose. The fragments of this object are no longer identifiable, but subsumed within the new, larger element, that itself begins to dissolve into the building which contains it. In the architect's words, the core's many guises are "rendered indivisible from the whole."[5] ■ Such indivisibility is by no means the end-all of some progressive search. It is merely evidence of one strain of the active experimentation in today's architectural practices, wherein architects are challenging the stale conventions that defined elemental forms, casting doubts as to the purity of

meaning? Likewise, can Donald Judd's works in Marfa, Texas, be understood as individual pieces without the presence of the rest of the collection or the building site around them [figures 7–8]? Such contextual factors are not simply spatial, but equally can be material, ethereal, social, or otherwise. Light, reflections, human behavior, production methods can all contribute to the ultimate consideration of an element's power to express ideas. In such cases, the artistry is as much *outside* the element as within it. ■ All of these considerations play out in the works presented across these pages, projects that challenge the terms of elements. Thus, a skylight in the Vancouver House by Patkau Architects doubles as a pool [figure 11, pages 94–97]; the superimposition allows each function to visually enrich its partner. For a house on the beach in Loveladies, New Jersey by Brian Healy, a metal column intertwines with a slatted wooden bench [pages 74–75]; the folded plane of the seatback both shelters the occupant and visually expresses the structural weight of the house's cantilevering volume. A display of polygonal shelves at Max Mara SoHo by Duccio Grassi Architects is formed from protruding drawers that can be slid back to create a solid wall of dark wood [pages 182–183]; their infinite oscillations produce a shopping experience in which the detail can change perpetually over time. The wooden clothing cases at Helmut Lang SoHo by Richard Gluckman are stripped of functional references and reconstituted through abstraction [pages 4–5]; the elements appear more like minimalist Donald Judd pieces than containers for retail

architectural elements as singular or irreducible forms. This climate of innovation opens new paths of thinking about elements as points of experimentation, contention, or surprise— and often in opposition to restrictive definitions of type-forms. ■ To this equation we might add one additional term of evolution. As much as elements shape the perception of the architecture around them, our perception of elements likewise is shaped by factors outside their surfaces. Elements often communicate with one another across a space, becoming moments of expression that together form a more complete argument. Although a similar process is certainly at work in the classical orders or the narrative of elements common to Scarpa's work, contemporary discourse has expanded the influence of such external factors on our conceptions of elements in unexpected ways. For instance, Gordon Matta-Clark's "Four Corners" recontextualizes generic fragments of a house's roof and walls [figure 6] to present the question: does the element itself carry meaning, or does its context dictate its

display. The entrance to Steven Holl's Chapel of St. Ignatius contains a pair of doors that are continuous components of the façade's wooden wall panel [pages 20–23]; a shotgunning of oval windows describes a pattern attuned not to the dimension of the doors, but to that of the larger wall surface. These skylight-pools, these bench-columns, these wall-shelves, these sculpture-displays, these window-door-walls intoxicate us, brewing a delirium of detail that enriches, and often controls, our experiences of each architectural environment. ■ As with many of the details in this book, these elements are small pieces of a building, yet they carry enormous conceptual weight; although they may serve commonplace functions, they are often infused with transcendent beauty, poetry, subversion, contradiction, narrative, or tension. Such elements create rewards in the small moments, discovering art in architecture's everyday components. Sylvia Plath observes a similar phenomenon in her poem "Black Rook in Rainy Weather." She writes: "Certain minor light may still lean incandescent out of kitchen table or chair, as if a celestial burning took possession of the most obtuse objects now and then—thus hallowing an interval otherwise inconsequent." She recalls that such moments have the power to "seize my senses" with "tricks of radiance"—yet the poem makes apparent that the radiance and tricks and celestial burnings are secondary to the singular word "my".[6] Nothing short of the presence of the observer gives such moments meaning. In much the same way, elements, at their most powerful, are signs of the architect's authorship, and they form the basis of a direct conversation between the designer and the observer. In doing so, they are meant to awaken something sensual in us. And the work to follow is presented with much the same thinking. These elements are objects to be consumed or studied, pieces for our sight and touch to devour. ■ In this manner, I am reminded of the work of an emerging artist, Mimi Moncier. Her paintings are catalogues of the various things around her, her immediate environment, her personal world, her persona. She creates documents—"scrapbooks" to use her term—that record her belongings with titles such as "My Lunch," "My Books," "My Library," "My Lingerie," "My Universe" [figure 9]. Each painting abstracts and distills the elements of her life, creating ringed figures of intense colors that float on fields of various shapes. In her words, these figures "act as focusing devices, like targets drawing the eyes irresistibly to the center, inviting them to gaze upon colors as objects of desire."[7] Such is our hope with this book: that you become *subject* to these *objects*. ■ All of this returns us to the idea of the catalogue.

gauges against which to measure the innovation, creativity, and complexity of the elements presented here. Where elements stray from this system, where they express their differences and uniqueness, where they resist categorization or show signs of "dangerous mixtures"—this is the defining moment that makes them worthy of our admiration.

Notes

1. Vitruvius, *The Ten Books on Architecture* (New York: Dover Publications, 1960), 75. ■ 2. Andrea Palladio, *The Four Books of Architecture* (New York: Dover Publications, 1965), 1. ■ 3. Marc-Antoine Laugier, *An Essay on Architecture* (Los Angeles: Hennessey & Ingalls, 1977), 3. ■ 4. Cited in *Carlo Scarpa Architect: Intervening with History* (New York: The Monacelli Press, 1992), 39; and originally quoted in *Carlo Scarpa* (Vincenza: Accademia Olimpica, 1974). ■ 5. Preston Scott Cohen, unpublished text provided by the architect. ■ 6. Sylvia Plath, "Black Rook in Rainy Weather," *The Collected Poems* (New York: HarperPerennial, 1992), 56–57. ■ 7. Mimi Moncier, unpublished statement provided by the artist. ■ 8. Michel Foucault, *The Order of Things* (New York: Vintage Books, 1994), xv.

Image Captions and Credits

Figure 1: Louis Kahn, Exeter Library, 1972; image courtesy Doug Dolezal. ■ Figure 2: Carlo Scarpa, Palazzo Querini

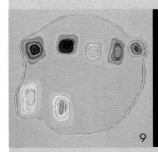
9

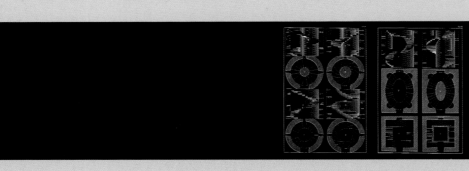
10

In his preface to *The Order of Things*, Michel Foucault offers a cautionary word on the subject. He recounts discovering a passage in Borges that quoted a "certain Chinese encyclopedia" of animal taxonomy, in which beasts were organized into exotic and absurd categories ranging from "embalmed" to "fabulous" and from "belonging to the Emperor" to "having just broken the water pitcher." For Foucault, the refreshing initial charm of this unusual system of classification faded quickly. It was replaced by concern for the specificity of the system and what it refused to imagine: "The possibility of dangerous mixtures had been exorcized…no inconceivable amphibious maidens, no clawed wings…" and so on.[8] In this, there is an echo of our own approach. ■ Despite the futility of our initial inclination to classify, we have treated this book as a catalogue of sorts—one that perhaps has more the opportunistic and pluralistic qualities of a scrapbook, and less the rigid insistence on consistency and absolutism. We have organized the projects into categories that we view as

Stampalia, 1963; image courtesy Eric Höweler. ■ Figures 3–4: Diller + Scofidio, Eyebeam Building, New York, 2002; images courtesy the architects. ■ Figure 5: Preston Scott Cohen, Torus House, 1999; image courtesy the architect. ■ Figure 6: Gordon Matta-Clark, "Four Corners," 1974; image © 2002 Estate of Gordon Matta-Clark/Artists Rights Society (ARS), New York. ■ Figure 7: Donald Judd, 100 untitled works in mill aluminum, 1982–1986. Chinati Foundation permanent collection, Marfa, Texas. Photography by Florian Holzherr. Judd art © Judd Foundation. ■ Figure 8: Donald Judd, untitled work in concrete, 1980–1984. Chinati Foundation permanent collection, Marfa, Texas. Photography by Florian Holzherr. Judd art © Judd Foundation. ■ Figure 9: Mimi Moncier, "My Lunch," 2002; image courtesy the artist. ■ Figure 10: Andrea Palladio, *The Four Books of Architecture* (New York: Dover Publications, 1965). ■ Figure 11: Patkau Architects, Vancouver House, 2002; image by Paul Warchol.

doors

"What should I turn to, lighting upon days like these? Every door is barr'd with gold, and opens but to golden keys," wrote Alfred, Lord Tennyson. ■ As an architectural element, the door suggests entry and opportunity, but also solidity and protection. ■ Today's architects are intent on exploring varied ideas of ingress and egress. ■ When or where is that gateway, that moment of entry, or exit? ■ Can or should the dichotomy between inside and outside be blurred, or even erased? ■ Robert Frost: "From the door I shall set forth for somewhere, I shall make the reckless choice."

Previous spread: Architecture Research Office, Capital Z Offices, New York, 1998. This spread: Pasanella + Klein Stolzman + Berg Architects, Fifth Avenue Residence, New York, 1989. The metal-framed door panels are positioned to structure the apartment's views of Central Park.

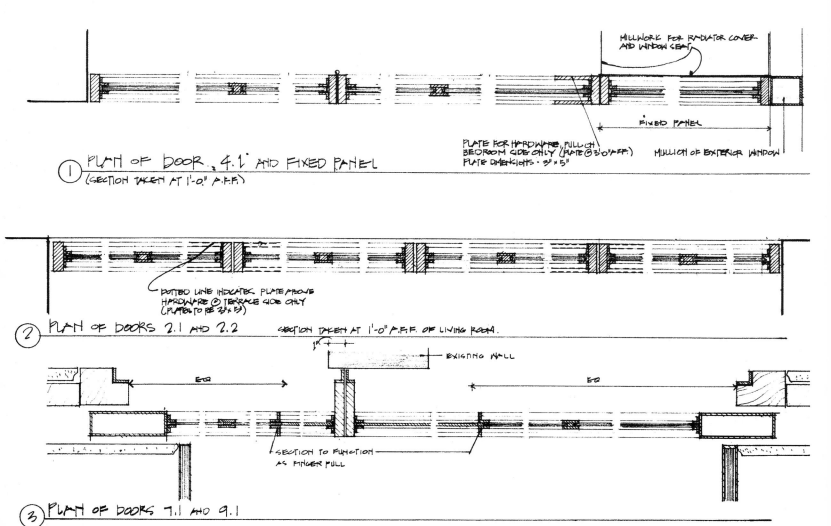

MILLWORK FOR RADIATOR COVER AND WINDOW SEAT

FIXED PANEL

PLATE FOR HARDWARE, PULL @ BEDROOM SIDE ONLY (PLATE @ 3'-0" A.F.F.) PLATE DIMENSIONS - 3" x 5"

MULLION OF EXTERIOR WINDOW

(1) PLAN OF DOOR 4.1 AND FIXED PANEL
(SECTION TAKEN AT 1'-0" A.F.F.)

DOTTED LINE INDICATES PLATE ABOVE HARDWARE @ TERRACE SIDE ONLY (PLATES TO BE 3" x 5")

(2) PLAN OF DOORS 2.1 AND 2.2   SECTION TAKEN AT 1'-0" A.F.F. OF LIVING ROOM.

EXISTING WALL

EQ

EQ

SECTION TO FUNCTION AS FINGER PULL

(3) PLAN OF DOORS 7.1 AND 9.1

Maya Lin Studio/David Hotson Architect, Upper East Side Residence, New York, 1999. Pivoting panels blur the distinction between doors and walls. The light color of the sycamore veneer paneling contrasts with darker strips along the floors and walls.

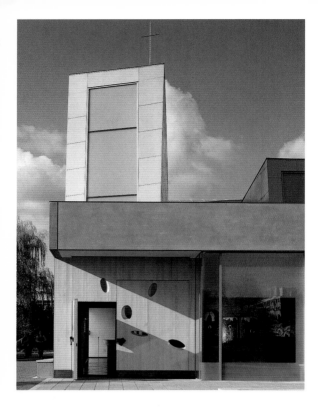

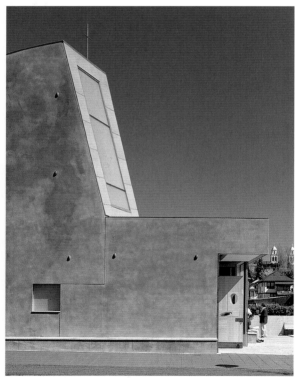

Previous spread: Steven Holl Architects, Chapel of St. Ignatius, Seattle, 1997. The hand-carved Alaskan yellow cedar doors are highlighted by bronze handles and punctured with oval windows of various shapes and sizes. This spread: Steven Holl Architects, Chapel of St. Ignatius, Seattle, 1997. The main door at the corner entrance faces a reflecting pond. The chapel is sited to form a new campus quadrangle.

Steven Holl Architects, Texas Stretto House, Dallas, 1992. An entrance door of weathered metal becomes part of a geometric composition also comprising glass and exterior concrete panels.

Craig Bassam Studio, Bally Caslano Headquarters, Caslano, Switzerland, 2000. The entire executive corridor is conceived as a series of equal panels, including the sliding oak doors. A simple curved detail on the door's edge suggests craft and handiwork, and visually differentiates the door when it is in its recessed position.

windows

If the eyes are the windows of the soul, then windows are the soul of a building. ■ Philip Larkin: "Rather than words comes the thought of high windows: The sun-comprehending glass, and beyond it, the deep blue air, that shows nothing, and is nowhere, and is endless . . ." ■ Windows are a transparent talisman, reconnecting a building's occupants to the air and light around them. ■ Sometimes they are part of a façade composition, sometimes they *are* the façade. ■ Either way, windows serve as the nexus between inside and outside, natural and machine-made, darkness and light.

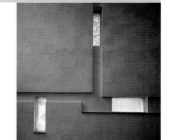

Previous spread: Steven Holl Architects, Chapel of St. Ignatius, Seattle, 1997. This spread: Brian Healy Architects (with Michael Ryan), Beach House, Loveladies, New Jersey, 1996. Four window groupings become part of a façade's geometric composition that also comprises sun-shading eaves and the house's service core.

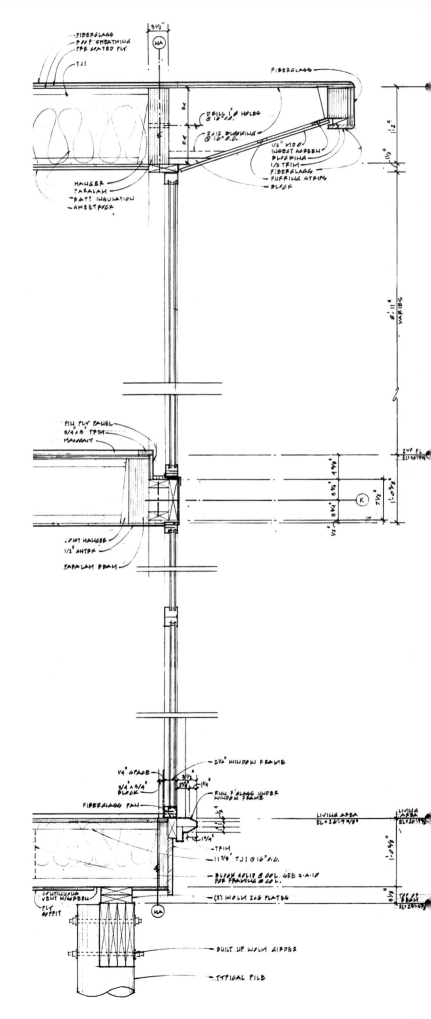

Maya Lin Studio/David Hotson Architect, Upper East Side Residence, New York, 1999. A two-level entrance hall in a townhouse, awash in natural light, can be opened to the master bedroom via a pivoting panel of sycamore veneer.

Steven Holl Architects, Y House, Upstate New York, 1999. Wings of the house meet at an obtuse angle, and the many windows are placed both to frame special views of the mountains and to maximize the amount of interior wall space devoted to artwork.

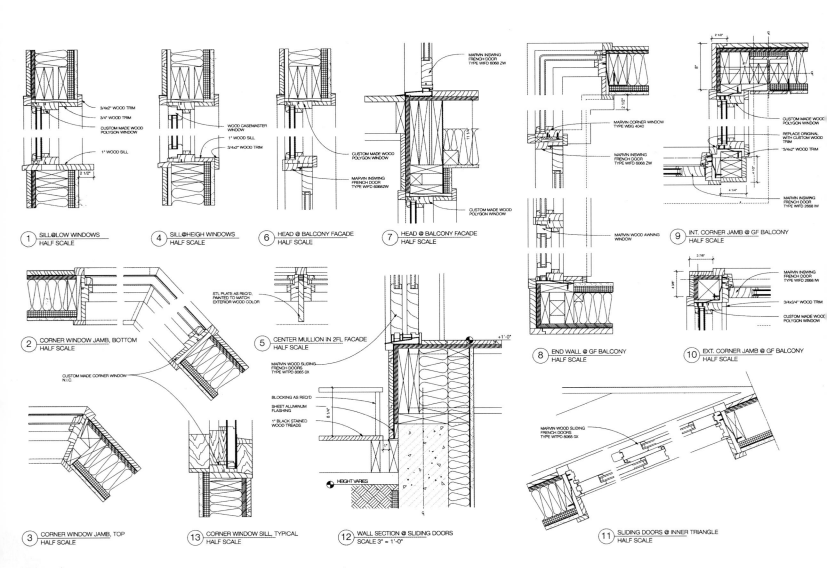

1 SILL @ LOW WINDOWS
HALF SCALE

4 SILL @ HEIGH WINDOWS
HALF SCALE

6 HEAD @ BALCONY FACADE
HALF SCALE

7 HEAD @ BALCONY FACADE
HALF SCALE

9 INT. CORNER JAMB @ GF BALCONY
HALF SCALE

2 CORNER WINDOW JAMB, BOTTOM
HALF SCALE

5 CENTER MULLION IN 2FL FACADE
HALF SCALE

8 END WALL @ GF BALCONY
HALF SCALE

10 EXT. CORNER JAMB @ GF BALCONY
HALF SCALE

3 CORNER WINDOW JAMB, TOP
HALF SCALE

13 CORNER WINDOW SILL, TYPICAL
HALF SCALE

12 WALL SECTION @ SLIDING DOORS
SCALE 3" = 1'-0"

11 SLIDING DOORS @ INNER TRIANGLE
HALF SCALE

Steven Holl Architects, Texas Stretto House, Dallas, 1992. The gentle spherical arc of the roof gives angular variety to the otherwise orthogonal composition of the house's large glass window compositions. Following spread: Steven Holl Architects, Bellevue Art Museum, Bellevue, Washington, 2001. The three distinct lighting conditions of the museum are visible through an internal window that is partly translucent.

Steven Holl Architects, Cranbrook Institute of Science, Bloomfield Hills, Michigan, 1999. A new entrance lobby forms a "Light Laboratory" with a south-facing wall of many types of glass. Different phenomena of light such as refraction and prismatic color are displayed on the lobby walls as the sunlight changes.

NBBJ, Teledesic Offices, Bellevue, Washington, 2000. In a renovated industrial building, large dormer-like "light monitors" and lower-level units of clear and frosted glass allow diffused northern light into the spaces.

walls

"Architects should strive to create a work . . . where the floor is the earth, the walls are the wind and the ceiling is the sky," said Richard England. ■ No element has undergone a more radical rethinking during the last century than the wall. ■ Liberated by modernists like Le Corbusier from being staid demarcations of rooms, walls have become angled and curved, transparent and translucent. ■ Today architects seek design approaches to enhance occupants' experience—planes intersect with each other and the ceiling in endless ways. ■ This is the wall as minimalist geometric art.

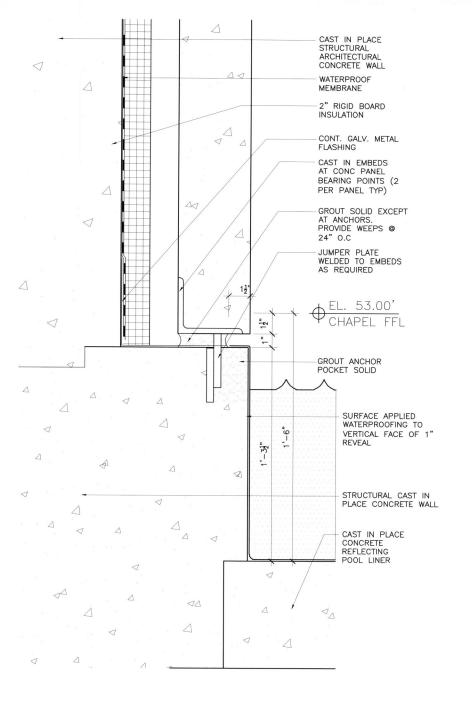

CAST IN PLACE
STRUCTURAL
ARCHITECTURAL
CONCRETE WALL

WATERPROOF
MEMBRANE

2" RIGID BOARD
INSULATION

CONT. GALV. METAL
FLASHING

CAST IN EMBEDS
AT CONC PANEL
BEARING POINTS (2
PER PANEL TYP)

GROUT SOLID EXCEPT
AT ANCHORS.
PROVIDE WEEPS @
24" O.C

JUMPER PLATE
WELDED TO EMBEDS
AS REQUIRED

EL. 53.00'
CHAPEL FFL

GROUT ANCHOR
POCKET SOLID

SURFACE APPLIED
WATERPROOFING TO
VERTICAL FACE OF 1"
REVEAL

STRUCTURAL CAST IN
PLACE CONCRETE WALL

CAST IN PLACE
CONCRETE
REFLECTING
POOL LINER

④ DETAIL PRECAST PANEL @ POOL

Previous spread: Peter Marino + Assoc Architects, Datascope Corporation, Mahwah, New Jersey, 2000. This spread: François de Menil, Architect, Byzantine Fresco Chapel Museum, Houston, 1997. Precast concrete panels vary in tone to provide depth and character to the façade, while a darkly colored pool maximizes reflection of the building on bright days.

Steven Holl Architects, Bellevue Art Museum, Bellevue, Washington, 2001. A range of natural and artificial light bathes the curvilinear walls of the museum.

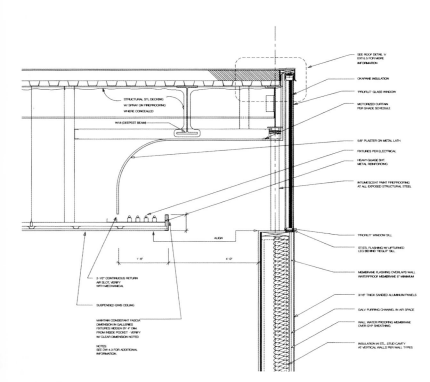

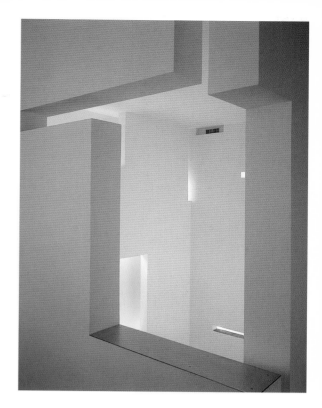

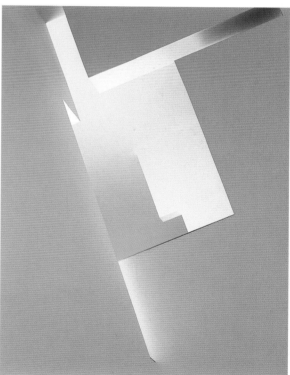

Steven Holl Architects, D.E. Shaw & Co. Offices, New York, 1992. The thirty-one-foot entrance cube is notched at strategic points, and color lights on the back or bottom surfaces of the notches mix with sunlight for ever-changing intersections of colors and geometric volumes.

Gluckman Mayner Architects, Mary Boone Gallery, New York, 1996. All visible surfaces are concrete and plaster, similarly finished and tinted light gray, producing an effect that blurs the distinction between floor, wall, and ceiling. The enlarged central column suggests a strong vertical axis in a predominantly horizontal space.

Smith-Miller + Hawkinson Architects, Private Residence, New York, 1997. Movable walls are placed at a variety of angles, allowing quick reconfiguration of a high-ceiling loft space. Following spread: Deborah Berke & Partners, Howell Loft, New York, 1999. The opening for a fireplace and a mantle form a simple geometric composition on a spare plaster wall.

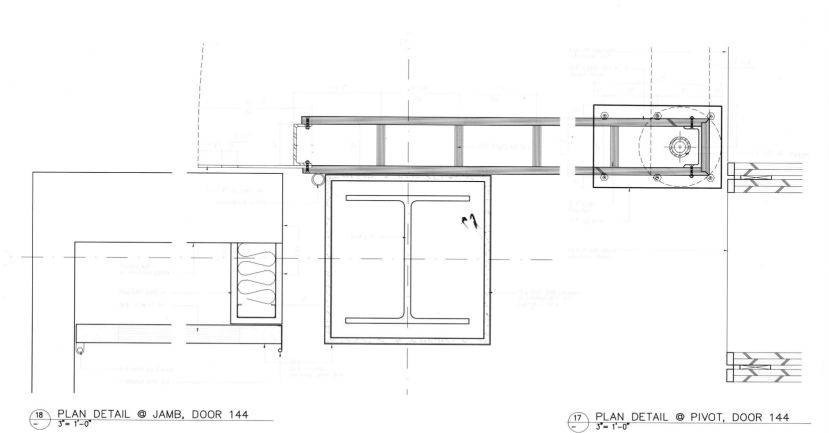

18 PLAN DETAIL @ JAMB, DOOR 144
3" = 1'-0"

17 PLAN DETAIL @ PIVOT, DOOR 144
3" = 1'-0"

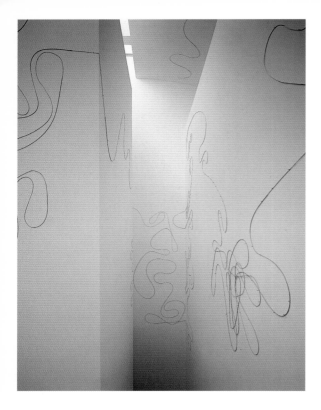

Olson Sundberg Kundig Allen Architects. Garden House, San Francisco Bay Area, 1998. An installation of natural objects by the sculptor Andy Goldsworthy enlivens the white walls in a stairwell of this private residence.

Office for Metropolitan Architecture/Rem Koolhaas and Architecture Research Office, Prada Store SoHo, New York, 2001. The translucent synthetic wall is illuminated from behind by windows and colored light fixtures. Its surface folds across the ceiling to form a glowing envelope around the space.

columns

"In the whole compass of the art of building, you will find nothing that deserves to be preferred before the columns," wrote Leon Battista Alberti. ■ Columns are at once pure function and pure form. ■ The great Greek and Roman architects obsessed over their proportions. ■ In the Renaissance they became architecture enlisted for transcendent purposes. ■ Twentieth-century masters used them to elevate buildings and free the ground plane. ■ However their forms now vary, columns can be thought of as architecture's version of nature's tree—strong, elegant, infinitely adaptable.

Previous spread: Daniel Rowen Architect, Martha Stewart Living/Omnimedia Offices, New York, 2001. This spread: Davis Brody Bond, Valeo Thermal Systems, North American Headquarters and Technical Center, Auburn Hills, Michigan, 1998. At once simple and grand, a system of louvers shades an exterior colonnade.

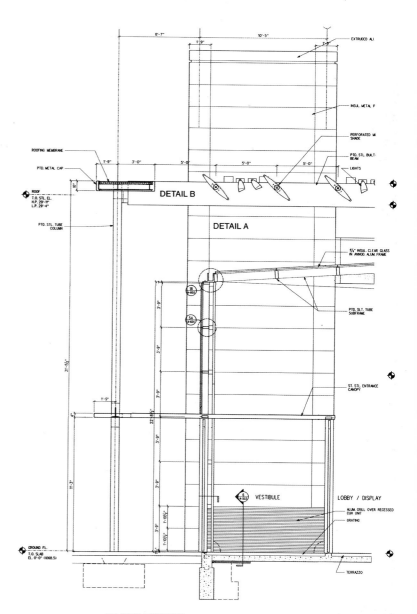

WALL SECTION @ LOBBY ENTRY
SCALE 1/2" = 1'-0"

Previous spread: Smith-Miller + Hawkinson Architects, North Carolina Museum of Art, Raleigh, North Carolina, 1997. An amphitheater and outdoor cinema feature columns splayed at various angles. This spread: Steven Holl Architects, Y House, Upstate New York, 1999. A twenty-first-century interpretation of the traditional domestic porch and balcony overlooks the Catskill Mountains.

Steven Holl Architects, Texas Stretto House, Dallas, 1992. Thin columns support curved roof sections, which in turn join the various wings of the house together.

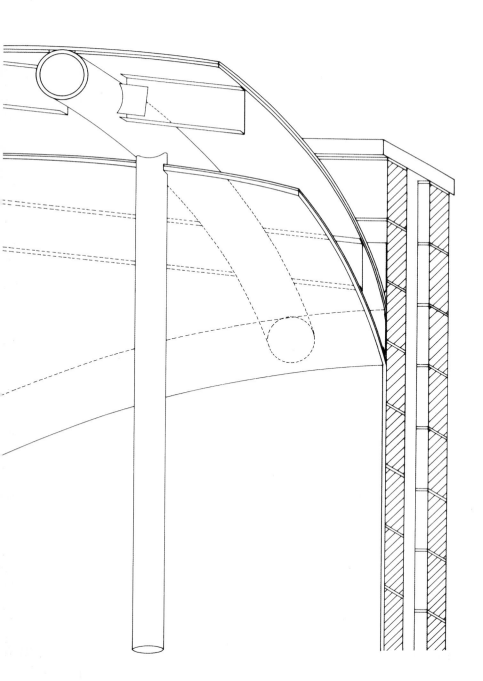

Steven Holl Architects, Makuhari Housing, Chiba, Japan, 1996. True to the modernist tradition, columns raise the entire structure and free the ground plane for plantings and habitable space. A set of stairs leads up from a garden court into the heart of a building, itself angled as if reaching skyward.

Brian Healy Architects (with Michael Ryan), Beach House, Loveladies, New Jersey, 1997. A column doubles as a wooden bench at this family beach house on the New Jersey shore.

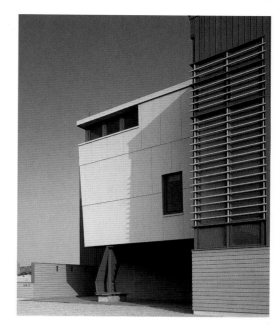

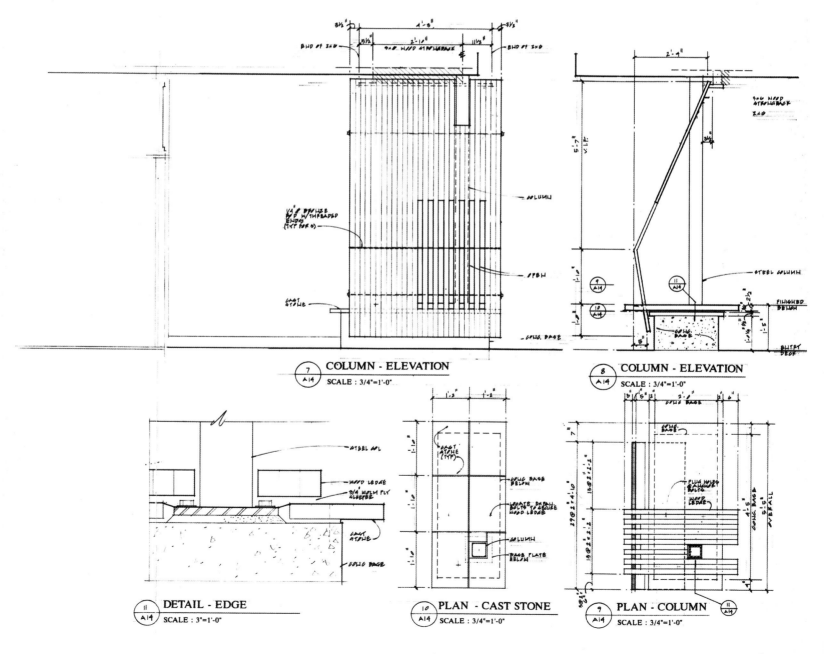

Maria Hellerstein and Nikolai Katz of HellKatz Architecture and Design, Starret LeHigh Building, New York, 2000. The free-form capitals in this office building lobby are of hand-fashioned plaster inspired by the shape of a calla lilly.

Deborah Berke & Partners, Howell Loft, New York, 1999.
A residential loft that doubles as a gallery, this live/work space
features columns with flared tops.

Daniel Rowen Architect, Martha Stewart Living/Omnimedia Offices, New York, 2001. A stately double colonnade defines this expansive, sun-washed place of work.

skylights

"More and more, it seems to me, light is the beautifier of the building," said Frank Lloyd Wright. ■ Indeed nothing brings a building's interior to life like natural light. ■ And yet the luminescence from a skylight is fundamentally different from that of a window. ■ It comes from above, a constant reminder to us earth-bound mortals that, to borrow E.B. White's paean to the New York skyscraper, "the way is up." ■ The skylight allows in a diffused glow that splashes onto walls, lightens otherwise obscure stairwells, throws dramatic shadows. ■ And it still keeps the rain out.

Previous spread: Steven Holl Architects, Chapel of St. Ignatius, Seattle, 1997. This spread: Steven Holl Architects, Museum of Contemporary Art, Helsinki, 1998. The architect's "bowtie" skylights appear to peel out from the curved metal roof, allowing natural light to filter down into the museum's galleries.

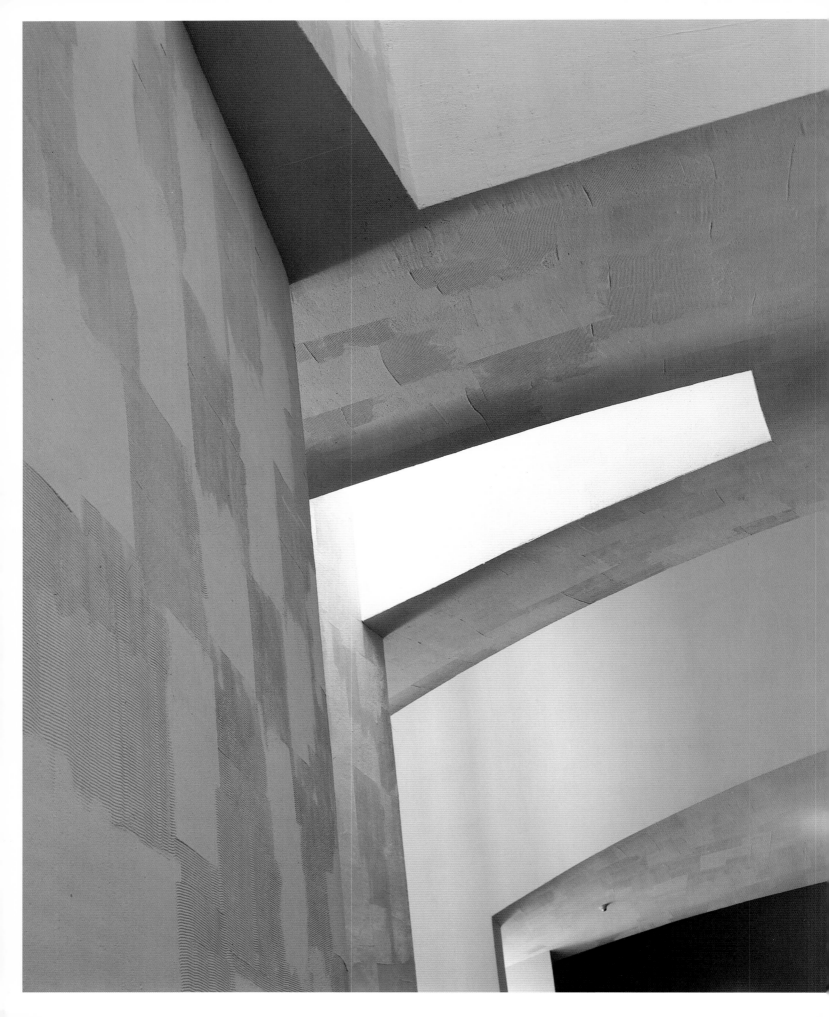

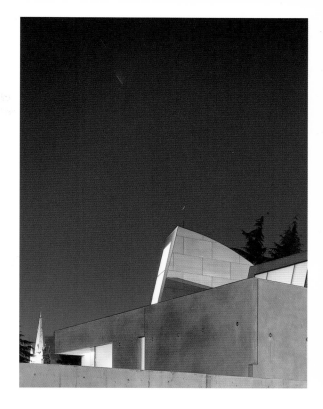

Previous spread: Steven Holl Architects, Chapel of St. Ignatius, Seattle, 1997. The sacred space is conceived as a series of light-filled volumes, and where volumes come together, there are skylights of various shapes, shedding light that is at once comforting and mysterious. This spread: Steven Holl Architects, Chapel of St. Ignatius, Seattle, 1997. Interior volumes of the chapel are bathed in colored light, although only the reflected color and not the skylight itself can be seen from within.

Steven Holl Architects, Bellevue Art Museum, Bellevue, Washington, 2001. In keeping with the "tripleness" that is the organizing theme of the building, skylights are designed to respond, in the architect's words, to the "three different conditions of time and light: Linear, Cyclic and Gnostic." Following spread: Steven Holl Architects, Sarphatistraat Offices, Amsterdam, 2000. The interior spaces are animated by "phenomenal screens of color." The screens form a spatial and experiential frame containing services, lighting, and air grilles.

Patkau Architects, Vancouver House, Vancouver, Canada, 2001. The lap pool on the west side of a private residence brings both daylight and artificial light reflected from the pool deep into the central area of the house.

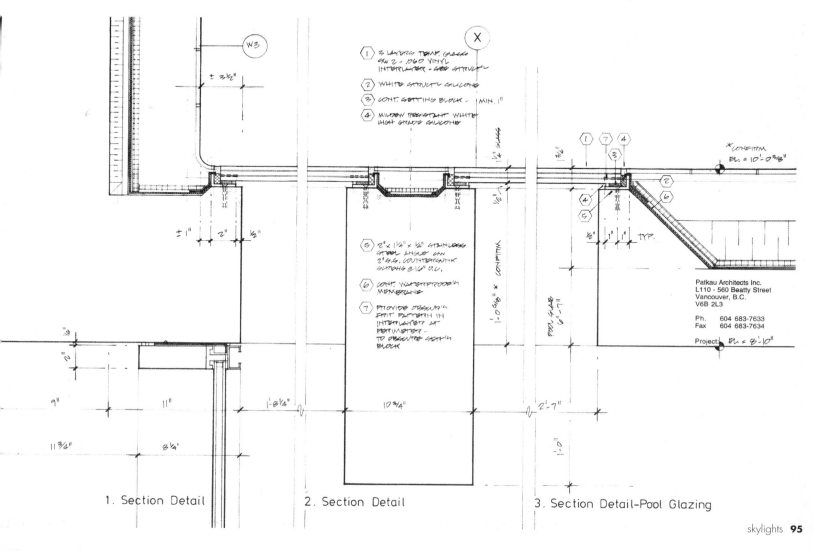

Patkau Architects Inc.
L110 - 560 Beatty Street
Vancouver, B.C.
V6B 2L3

Ph.   604 683-7633
Fax   604 683-7634

1. Section Detail   2. Section Detail   3. Section Detail-Pool Glazing

Patkau Architects, Vancouver House, Vancouver, Canada, 2001. Diaphanous reflections from the pool turn an ordinary wall into an ever-changing mural of light.

canopies

From Bernini's effusive *Baldacchino* in St. Peter's Basilica to the silk-lined rooms of royalty, a canopy denotes importance. "Here and nowhere else," it announces, is an entrance, an altar, a king's throne. ■ The canopy can also serve as the point of transition between inside and out. ■ It can test the architect's engineering daring—the cantilevered canopy over a main entrance provides protection against the elements. ■ But such a structure also seems to float effortlessly, almost magically, as if suspended from the sky, under what William Shakespeare lyrically called "this fair canopy of stars."

Previous, this, and following spreads: Davis Brody Bond, U.S. Bureau of the Census, Administration and Data Processing Headquarters, Bowie, Maryland, 1998. Fin-shaped steel brackets with cables lend a high-tech ambience to this government complex.

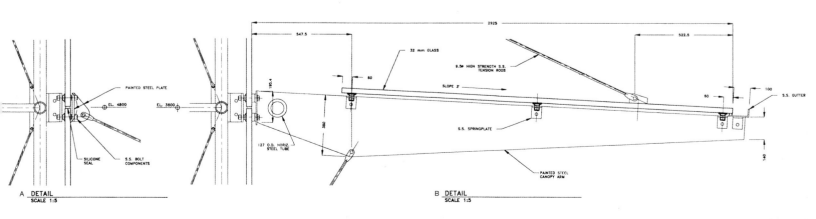

A DETAIL
   SCALE 1:5

B DETAIL
   SCALE 1:5

Steven Holl Architects, Cranbrook Institute of Science, Bloomfield Hills, Michigan, 1999. A riveted steel canopy defines the addition's new entrance lobby, which forms a "Light Laboratory" with a south-facing wall that is constructed from several types of glass.

Parsons + Fernandez-Casteleiro, Architects, Brooklyn Botanical Gardens, Horticultural Services Building, 1998. A galvanized steel canopy with angular supports defines the structure's main façade.

Olson Sundberg Kundig Allen Architects, Private Residence, Seattle, 2002. An off-center pivoting door of blackened steel leads to an interior entrance canopy of the same material, designed to achieve a warm patina with age.

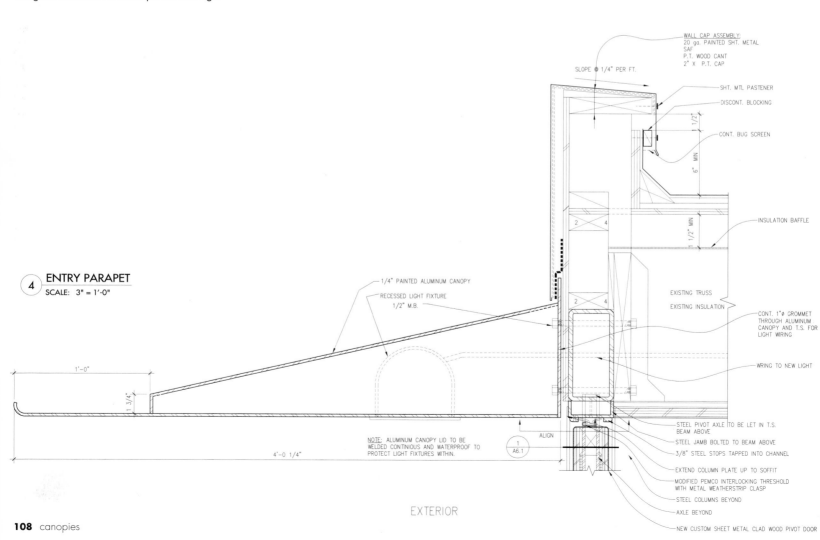

④ **ENTRY PARAPET**
SCALE: 3" = 1'-0"

WALL CAP ASSEMBLY;
20 ga. PAINTED SHT. METAL
SAF
P.T. WOOD CANT
2" X P.T. CAP

SLOPE @ 1/4" PER FT.

SHT. MTL PASTENER

DISCONT. BLOCKING

CONT. BUG SCREEN

INSULATION BAFFLE

1/4" PAINTED ALUMINUM CANOPY

RECESSED LIGHT FIXTURE
1/2" M.B.

EXISTING TRUSS

EXISTING INSULATION

CONT. 1"ø GROMMET
THROUGH ALUMINUM
CANOPY AND T.S. FOR
LIGHT WIRING

WRING TO NEW LIGHT

ALIGN

STEEL PIVOT AXLE ITO BE LET IN T.S.
BEAM ABOVE

STEEL JAMB BOLTED TO BEAM ABOVE

3/8" STEEL STOPS TAPPED INTO CHANNEL

NOTE; ALUMINUM CANOPY LID TO BE
WELDED CONTINIOUS AND WATERPROOF TO
PROTECT LIGHT FIXTURES WITHIN.

EXTEND COLUMN PLATE UP TO SOFFIT

MODIFIED PEMCO INTERLOCKING THRESHOLD
WITH METAL WEATHERSTRIP CLASP

STEEL COLUMNS BEYOND

AXLE BEYOND

NEW CUSTOM SHEET METAL CLAD WOOD PIVOT DOOR

EXTERIOR

stairs

"All rising to a great place is by a winding stair," said Francis Bacon. ■ A staircase speaks to the human need for ritual—arrive, ascend, enter. ■ Rising into a building or within its interior spaces can be accomplished by other means, but none as suffused with a sense of procession and drama. ■ The ancient Greeks and Romans used the staircase as the center of ritual; the Renaissance, as the metaphor for celestial striving; the *Beaux-Arts,* as an elaborate stage set; the Bauhaus, as an essential building element whose appearance perfectly matched its task.

Previous spread: Architecture Research Office, Colorado House, Telluride, Colorado, 1999. This spread: Patkau Architects, Vancouver House, Vancouver, Canada, 2001. The treads of the stairs become part of the geometric play among the house's walls and windows.

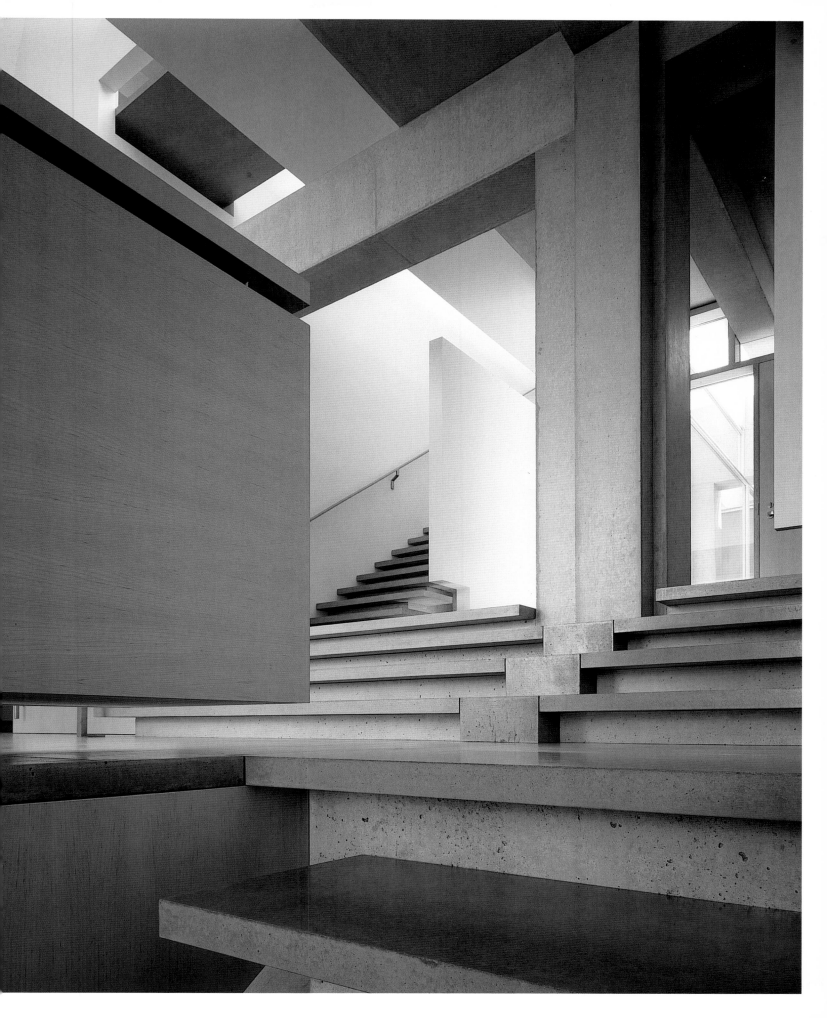

Olson Sundberg Kundig Allen Architects, Mission Hill Family Estate Winery, Westbank, British Columbia, 2001. For a spiral staircase leading up the winery's bell tower, there is a central concrete core around which the stairs are arrayed. Each stair is 3/16 of an inch narrower than the one below it so the spiral gently tapers as it goes up.

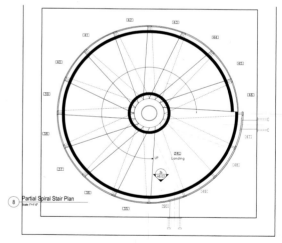

Partial Spiral Stair Plan
Scale 1"=1'-0"

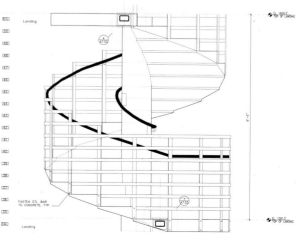

FASTEN STL. BAR
TO CONCRETE, TYP.

Gabellini Associates, Jil Sander Showroom, Milan, 2000. A staircase is defined in part by ethereal glass railings. Following spread: Gabellini Associates, Jil Sander Showroom, Milan, 2000. This wide processional stairway forms a stage inside the fashion showroom.

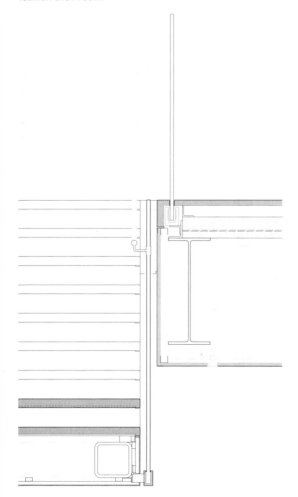

Jay Smith in collaboration with Michael Gabellini of Gabellini Associates, West 12th Street Residence, New York, 1989. A white marble stair comprises individual rectangular volumes that appear to hover unsupported.

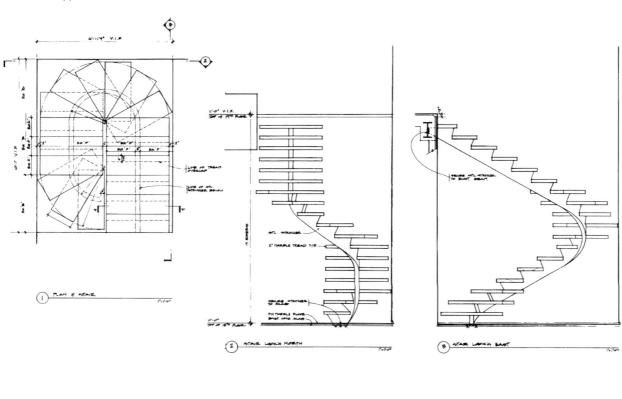

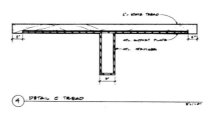

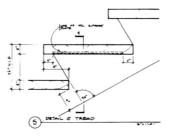

Shelton, Mindel & Associates, Manhattan Rooftop Residence, New York, 1997. A sinuous, curving set of stairs contrasts sharply with the adjacent angular glass screen partitions.

Architecture Research Office, SoHo Loft, New York, 1999. The treads of the loft's stairway seem suspended from metal railings.

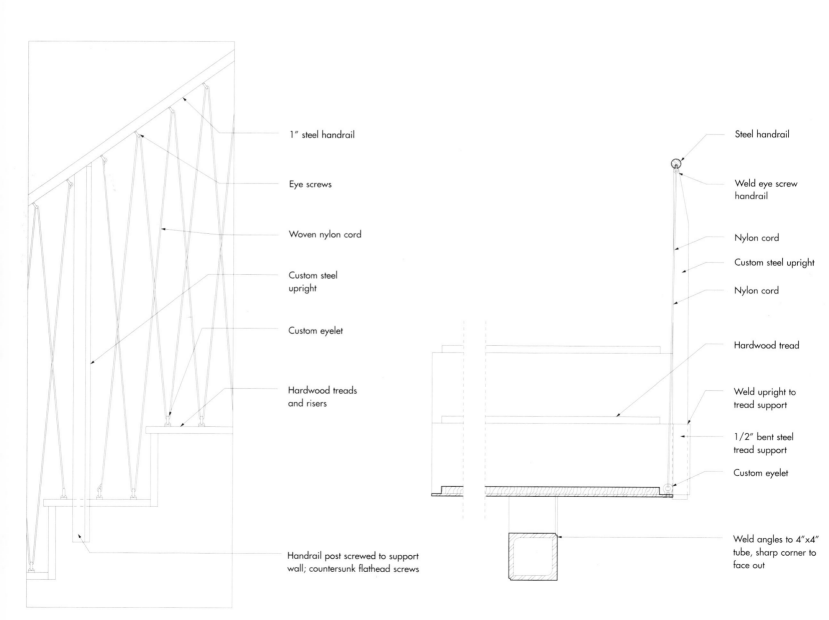

1" steel handrail

Eye screws

Woven nylon cord

Custom steel upright

Custom eyelet

Hardwood treads and risers

Handrail post screwed to support wall; countersunk flathead screws

Steel handrail

Weld eye screw handrail

Nylon cord

Custom steel upright

Nylon cord

Hardwood tread

Weld upright to tread support

1/2" bent steel tread support

Custom eyelet

Weld angles to 4"x4" tube, sharp corner to face out

Architecture Research Office, SoHo Loft, New York, 1999. A second stairway in the loft seems a cascade suspended in a sheet of glass. Its stainless steel tube risers are connected by milled aluminum subtreads, which are capped by horizontal planes of oak that function as the stair's walking surface.

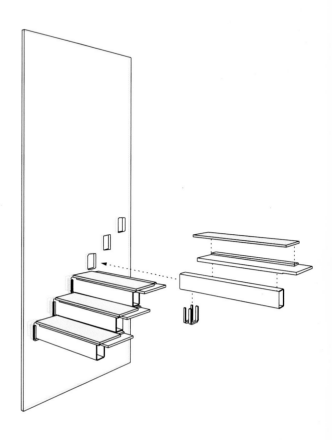

Architecture Research Office, SoHo Loft, New York, 1999. The architects took special care with the point at which the stair's milled aluminum brackets meet the laminated glass wall.

1 Stair #3 - East Elevation/Section
   1/2"=1'-0"

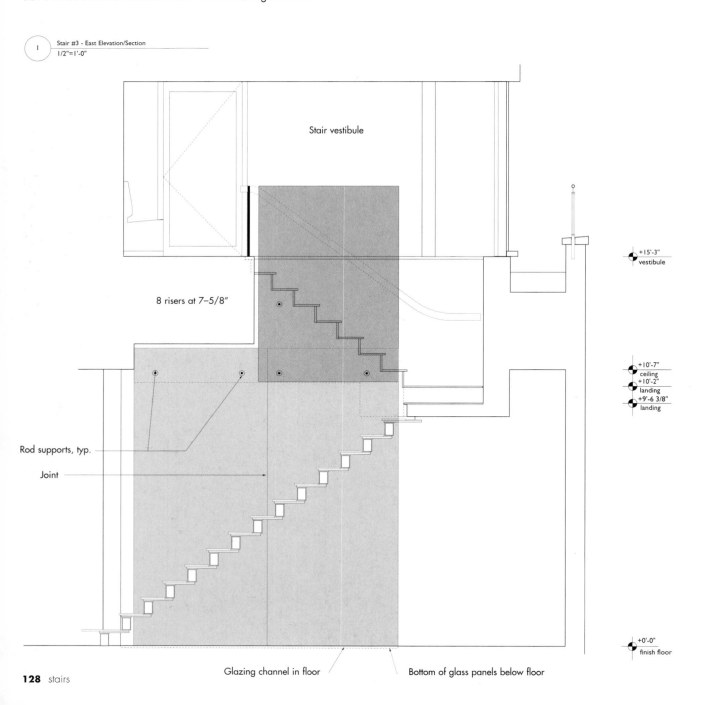

Stair vestibule

8 risers at 7–5/8"

Rod supports, typ.

Joint

+15'-3"
vestibule

+10'-7"
ceiling
+10'-2"
landing
+9'-6 3/8"
landing

+0'-0"
finish floor

Glazing channel in floor

Bottom of glass panels below floor

Krueck & Sexton Architects, Stainless Steel Apartment, Chicago, 1994. In an apartment building designed by Mies van der Rohe, the architects make a nod to the modernist master with a set of boldly cantilevered stairs in stainless steel.

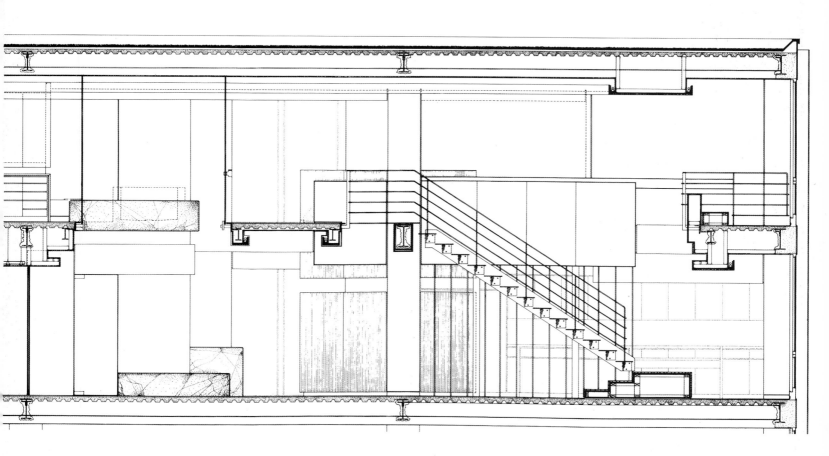

railings

Railings are architecture's most tactile element, the point at which we come in the closest physical contact with a building. ■ If the railing is made of wood, it feels warm and porous, a welcome intervention of nature against otherwise man-made materials; if of brushed stainless steel, it is often cool and silky to the touch. ■ A railing organizes interior space, sometimes gently, other times more brusquely. ■ It can act as a stern barrier offering absolute protection from gravity, or a more delicate structure, as if daring the user to test its strength. ■ The result: a unique intimacy between element and user.

Previous spread: Barkow Leibinger Architects, Trumpf Customer and Training Center, Farmington, Connecticut, 1999. This spread: Patkau Architects, Vancouver House, Vancouver, Canada, 2001. A bridge traverses a space, and a sheet of glass acts both as transparent wall and guardrail.

Gabellini Associates, Jil Sander Showroom, Milan, 2000. The brushed stainless steel handrail appears weightless, floating on exacting planes of glass that form the railing along the stairway.

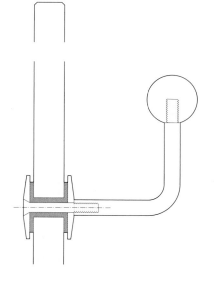

Machado and Silvetti Associates, Lippincott & Margulies Offices, New York, 1998. Frameless panels of milky glass line the staircase between the firm's upper and lower levels.

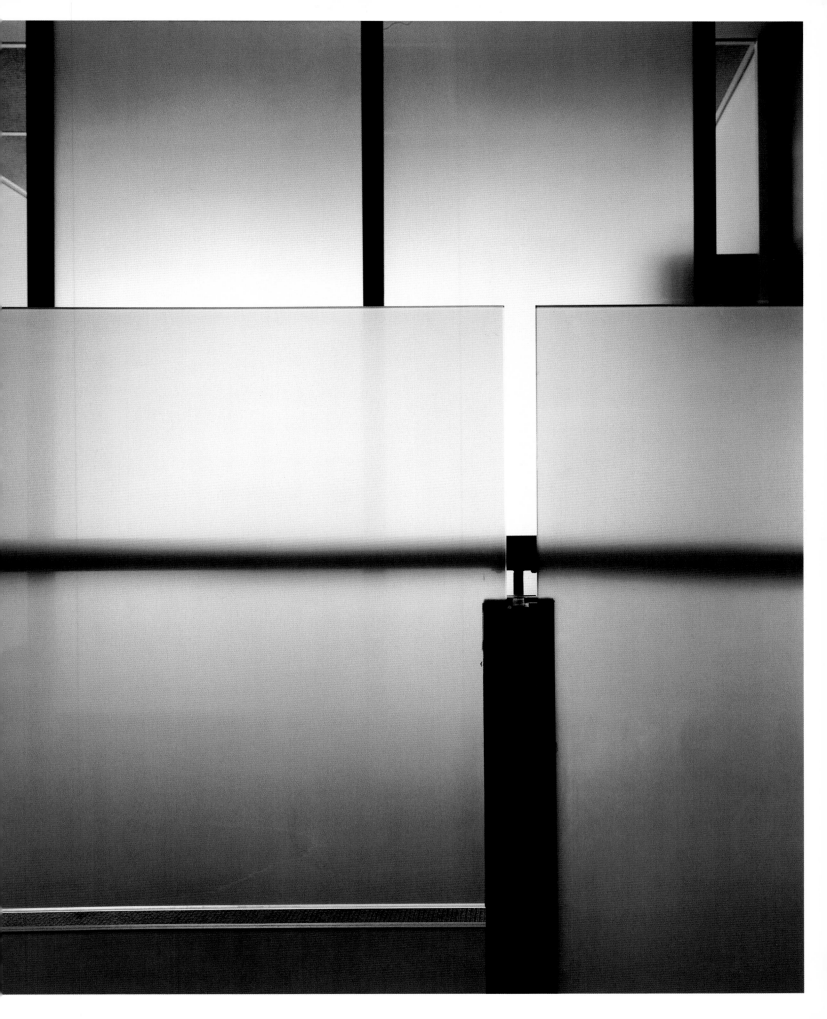

Architecture Research Office, SoHo Loft, New York, 1999. The treads and risers are anchored on one end in a glass wall and on the other by cables suspended from the sensuously shaped metal handrail.

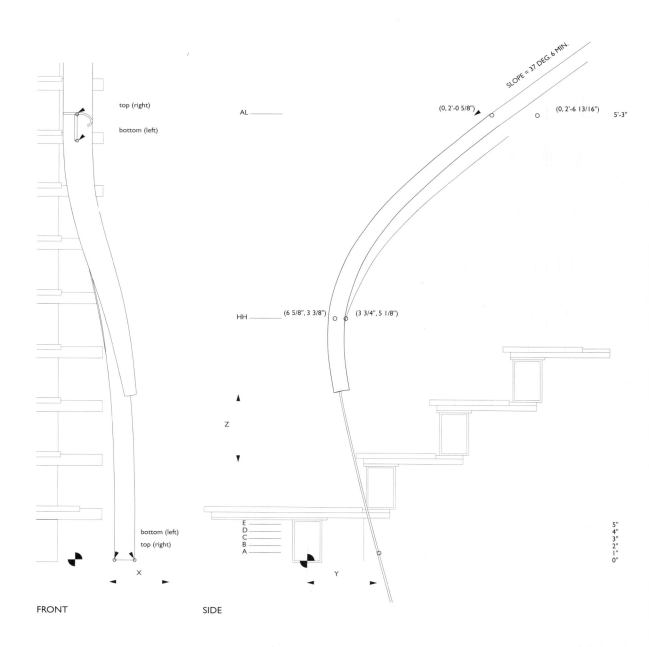

top (right)

bottom (left)

SLOPE = 37 DEG. 6 MIN.

AL

(0, 2'-0 5/8")

(0, 2'-6 13/16")

5'-3"

HH

(6 5/8", 3 3/8")

(3 3/4", 5 1/8")

Z

bottom (left)

top (right)

E
D
C
B
A

X

Y

5"
4"
3"
2"
1"
0"

FRONT

SIDE

Hariri & Hariri, Fifth Avenue Apartment, New York, 1998. A stairway has cantilevered treads without risers, and is visually anchored by a simple, brushed stainless steel railing.

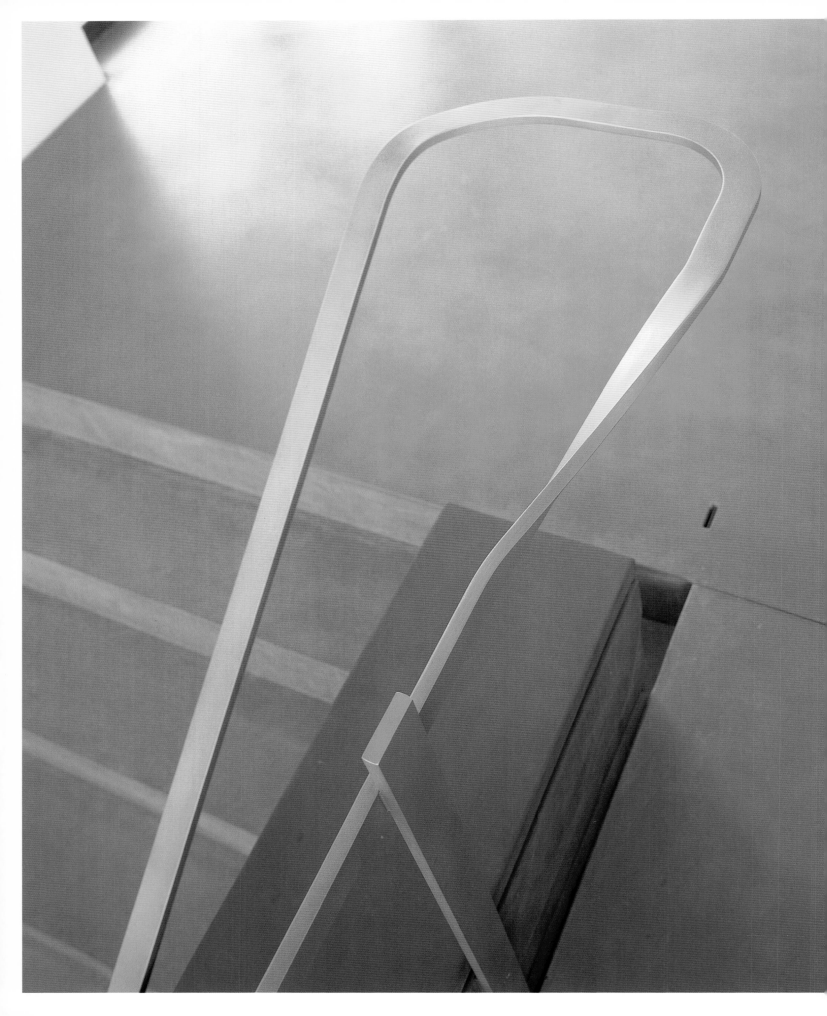

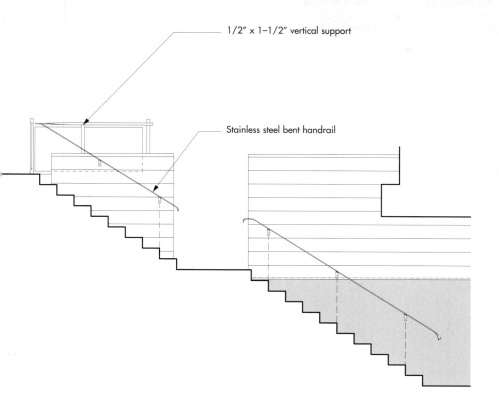

1/2" x 1-1/2" vertical support

Stainless steel bent handrail

Architecture Research Office, Colorado House, Telluride, Colorado, 1999. In an elegant and deft gesture of architectural calisthenics, a brushed stainless steel handrail transforms itself into a vertical guardrail with a simple twist. Following spread: Maya Lin Studio/David Hotson Architect, Upper East Side Residence, New York, 1999. An outline of blackened steel provides the principal structure of this stair, which is composed of vertical steel rods that are anchored in the railing supporting "sandwiches" of 3/8 inch plates of wood and blackened steel.

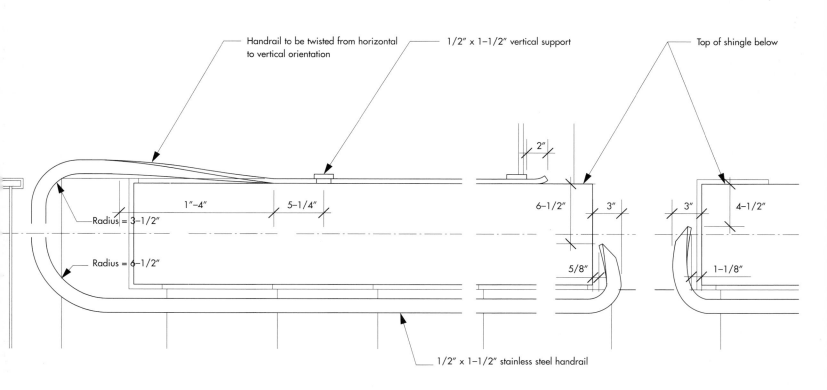

Handrail to be twisted from horizontal to vertical orientation

1/2" x 1-1/2" vertical support

Top of shingle below

1"-4"

5-1/4"

2"

6-1/2"

3"

3"

4-1/2"

Radius = 3-1/2"

Radius = 6-1/2"

5/8"

1-1/8"

1/2" x 1-1/2" stainless steel handrail

Steven Holl Architects, Bellevue Art Museum, Bellevue, Washington, 2001. The museum comprises three gallery lofts connected by a stair with wide treads and shallow risers that are defined in part by brushed stainless steel railings. The far railing does an adroit twist to become a vertical support.

Steven Holl Architects, Y House, Upstate New York, 1999. Like the house itself, the stair forms a "Y" in plan, and its dark metal railings help organize the unconventionally shaped interior spaces.

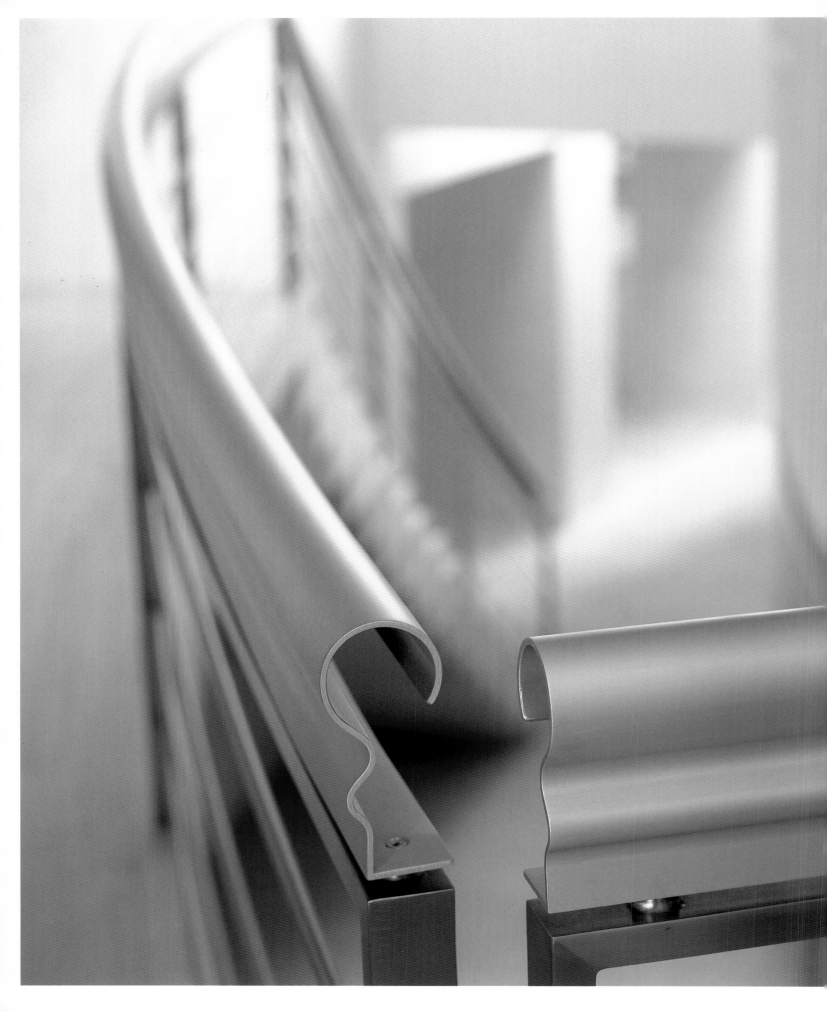

Peter L. Gluck and Partners, Architects, Residence in Highland Park, Illinois, 1998. The break in a curved aluminum railing reveals the question-mark shape from which it is extruded. The upper aluminum element is bolted to stainless steel railing components.

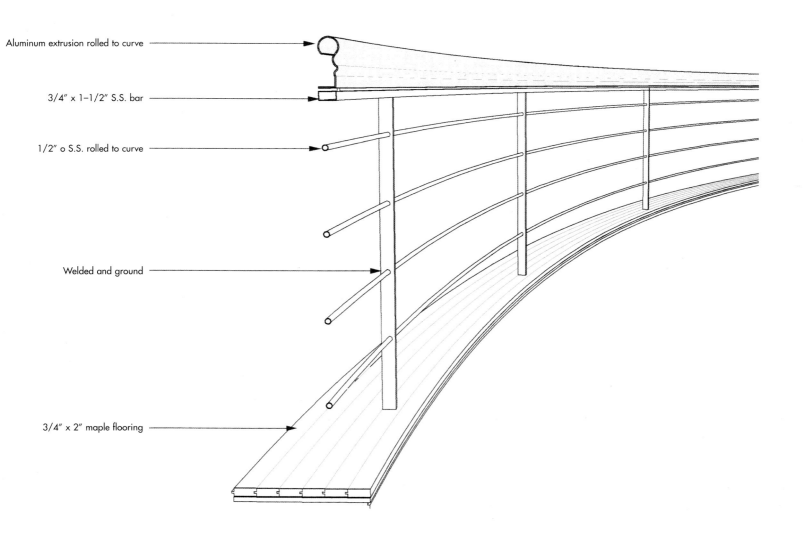

Aluminum extrusion rolled to curve

3/4" x 1-1/2" S.S. bar

1/2" o S.S. rolled to curve

Welded and ground

3/4" x 2" maple flooring

Eric J. Cobb Architect, Cirone Brannon House, Seattle, 1999. The parts of the stair are conceived as separate elements—a metal handrail for support and a sheet of glass as a security barrier. Given their different uses, the elements are thus set on different planes.

Ogawa/Depardon Architects, Upper East Side Townhouse, New York, 1998. The handrail is warm maple in an extruded oval form and is connected to a stainless steel railing structure. The stairwell is lit from a skylight above and from the translucent panels of adjacent rooms.

Gary Shoemaker Architects, Transitional Services for New York, Queens, New York, 2001. A building five feet below grade results in a "moat" which is in turn protected by a brushed aluminum and glass railing that matches the building's modernist façade. The railing's transparency prevents a forbidding institutional look in the complex's largely residential Queens setting.

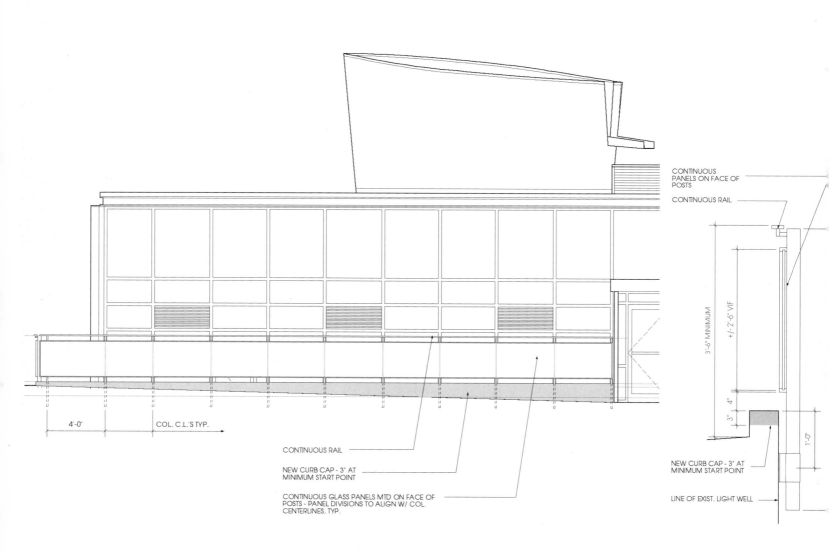

CONTINUOUS PANELS ON FACE OF POSTS

CONTINUOUS RAIL

3'-6" MINIMUM

+/- 2'-6" VIF

4"

3"

1'-0"

4'-0"

COL. C.L.'S TYP.

CONTINUOUS RAIL

NEW CURB CAP - 3" AT MINIMUM START POINT

CONTINUOUS GLASS PANELS MTD ON FACE OF POSTS - PANEL DIVISIONS TO ALIGN W/ COL. CENTERLINES, TYP.

NEW CURB CAP - 3" AT MINIMUM START POINT

LINE OF EXIST. LIGHT WELL

1 PARTIAL ELEVATION: RAILING CONFIGURATION, TYP.
1/4" = 1'-0"

2 DETAIL SECTION
1" = 1'-0"

screens

Traditional folding screens from Japan—known as *byobu*, literally meaning "protection from wind"—were developed to be dividers, both inside and out. ■ In modern parlance the indoor screen is a wall unwilling to make a commitment. ■ But it is this versatility and mobility that bring screens to the forefront of today's designers' repertoires. ■ Furthering screens' usefulness is the wide variety of materials that can make them semi-transparent, translucent, opaque—teasing us with a faint image of what is going on behind them. ■ The screen is an architectural element holding an element of mystery.

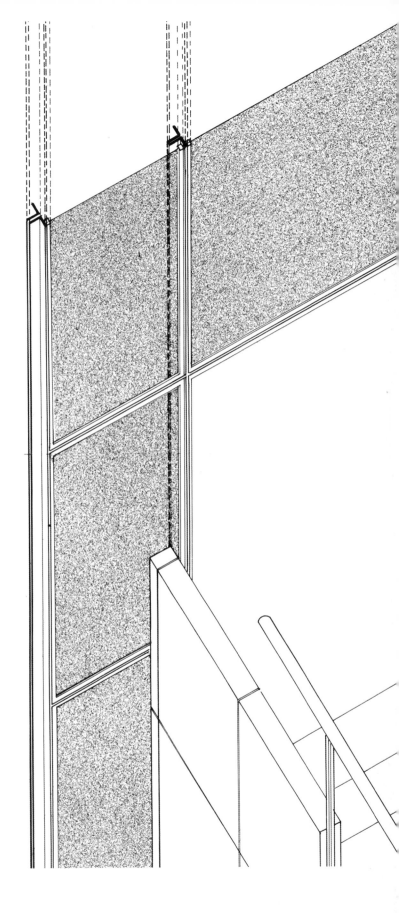

Previous spread: Gensler San Francisco, Management Consulting Offices, 2002. This spread: Pasanella + Klein Stolzman + Berg Architects, Root House, Ormand Beach, Florida, 1995. A glass and steel screen adjacent to a bridge delineates the public and private portions of the house.

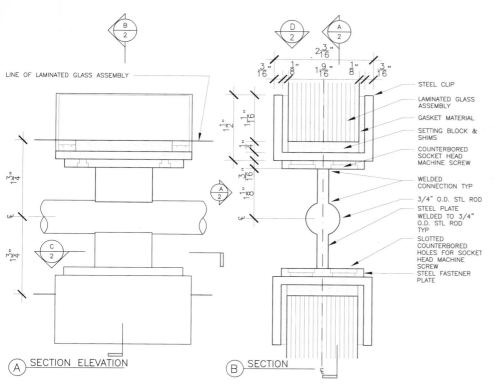

LINE OF LAMINATED GLASS ASSEMBLY

STEEL CLIP

LAMINATED GLASS ASSEMBLY

GASKET MATERIAL

SETTING BLOCK & SHIMS

COUNTERBORED SOCKET HEAD MACHINE SCREW

WELDED CONNECTION TYP

3/4" O.D. STL ROD

STEEL PLATE WELDED TO 3/4" O.D. STL ROD TYP

SLOTTED COUNTERBORED HOLES FOR SOCKET HEAD MACHINE SCREW

STEEL FASTENER PLATE

2 3/16"

3/16" 1/8" 1 9/16" 1/8" 3/16"

1 1/2" 1 1/16"

1" 1/16" 3/16" 1"

1 3/4"

1 3/4"

Ⓐ SECTION ELEVATION

Ⓑ SECTION

② TYPICAL HORIZONTAL/VERTICAL ROD CLIP DETAIL

François de Menil, Architect, Byzantine Fresco Chapel Museum, Houston, 1997. The screen is composed of multiple panels of frosted glass joined to recall vaulting and other elements of Byzantine architecture.

Krueck & Sexton Architects, Stainless Steel Apartment, Chicago, 1994. In an apartment building designed by Mies van der Rohe, a minimalist louvered screen stands adjacent to the cantilevered stainless steel stairway. Following spread: CR Studio Architects, Eileen Fisher Showroom, New York, 1997. A screen with frosted and clear glass becomes a Mondrianesque interior element, as if it were a reductive sculpture that separates the two rooms.

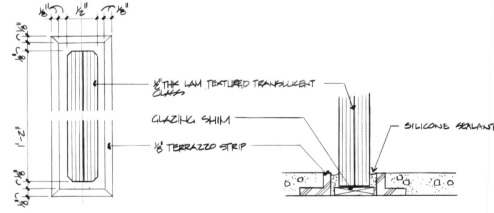

⅛" THK LAM TEXTURED TRANSLUCENT GLASS

GLAZING SHIM

⅛" TERRAZZO STRIP

SILICONE SEALANT

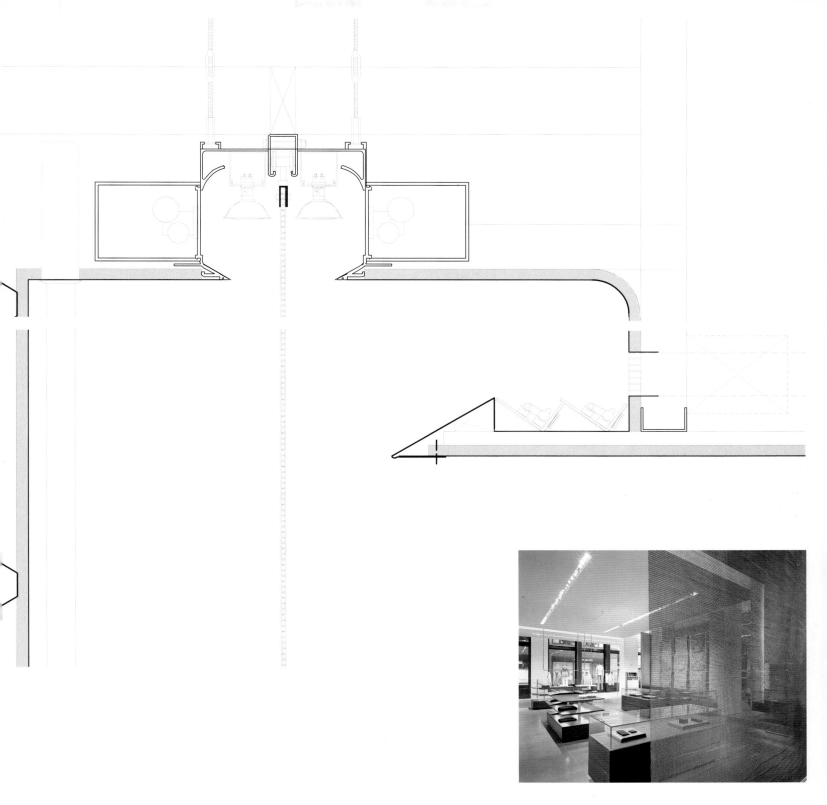

Gabellini Associates, Salvatore Ferragamo Boutique SoHo, New York, 2001. A woven metal screen of nickel-silver chain mail lends a hint of mystery to a retail store's merchandising.

TEN Arquitectos, Princeton Parking Garage, Princeton, New Jersey, 2000. Horizontal rods and woven vertical cables form a stainless steel curtain that sheathes the outside of the garage.

Davis Brody Bond, Valeo Thermal Systems, North American Headquarters and Technical Center, Auburn Hills, Michigan, 1998. Above a colonnade, louvers installed at a carefully calculated angle mitigate heat gain on the southern curtain wall.

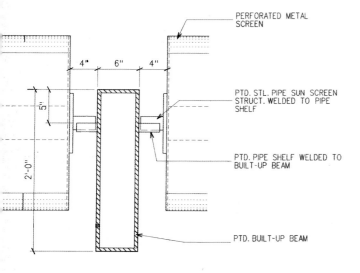

PERFORATED METAL SCREEN

PTD. STL. PIPE SUN SCREEN STRUCT. WELDED TO PIPE SHELF

PTD. PIPE SHELF WELDED TO BUILT-UP BEAM

PTD. BUILT-UP BEAM

4" 6" 4"

5"

2'-0"

B SECTION DETAIL @ SUN SCREEN
SCALE: 1½" · 1'-0"

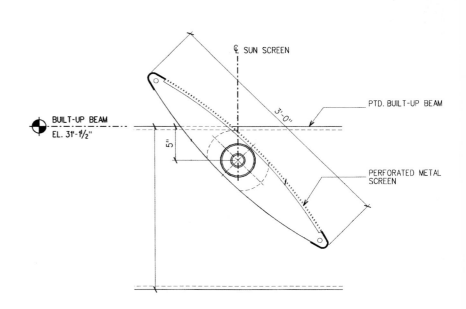

₵ SUN SCREEN

BUILT-UP BEAM
EL. 31'-1½"

PTD. BUILT-UP BEAM

PERFORATED METAL SCREEN

3'-0"

5"

A SECTION DETAIL @ SUN SCREEN
SCALE: 1½" · 1'-0"

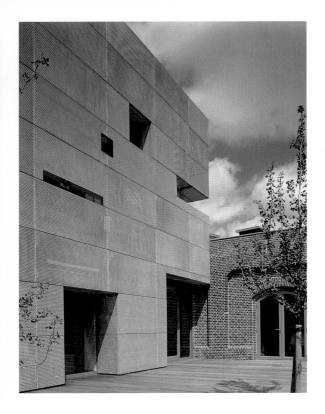

Steven Holl Architects, Sarphatistraat Offices, Amsterdam, 2000. Exterior screens form a spatial and experiential frame that contrasts sharply with the traditional brick architecture of Amsterdam, while at the same time housing services such as lighting and air grilles.

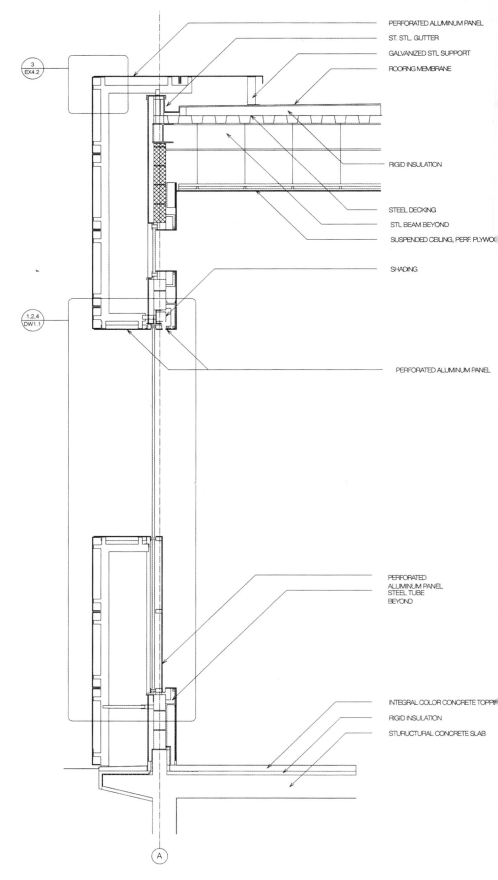

PERFORATED ALUMINUM PANEL
ST. STL. GUTTER
GALVANIZED STL SUPPORT
ROOFING MEMBRANE

RIGID INSULATION

STEEL DECKING
STL BEAM BEYOND
SUSPENDED CEILING, PERF. PLYWOOD

SHADING

PERFORATED ALUMINUM PANEL

PERFORATED
ALUMINUM PANEL
STEEL TUBE
BEYOND

INTEGRAL COLOR CONCRETE TOPPING
RIGID INSULATION
STURUCTURAL CONCRETE SLAB

Steven Holl Architects, Makuhari Housing, Chiba, Japan, 1996. A variety of building elements exists one layer behind the perforated metal panels.

cabinetry

The word "cabinet" originally referred to a small, ornate room for the display of personal treasures—"Who so views my cabinet's rich store is travel'd through the world, and some part more," wrote Henry Adamson. ■ The word eventually came to mean stand-alone furniture, but early modernists like Loos and Mackintosh fused building with furnishings, taking special care with built-in cabinetry. ■ Architects now are exploring new ways to continue this marriage of the practical and the aesthetic, lavishing particular attention on hardware—hinges and handles, often treasures in themselves.

Previous spread: Peter L. Gluck and Partners, Architects, Residence in Highland Park, Illinois, 1998. This spread: Duccio Grassi Architects, Max Mara SoHo, New York, 2001. A creative melding of two cabinetry elements: upon descending the store's staircase, customers view a wood display wall on which polygonal shelves, equipped with lights on their undersides, pop out like drawers.

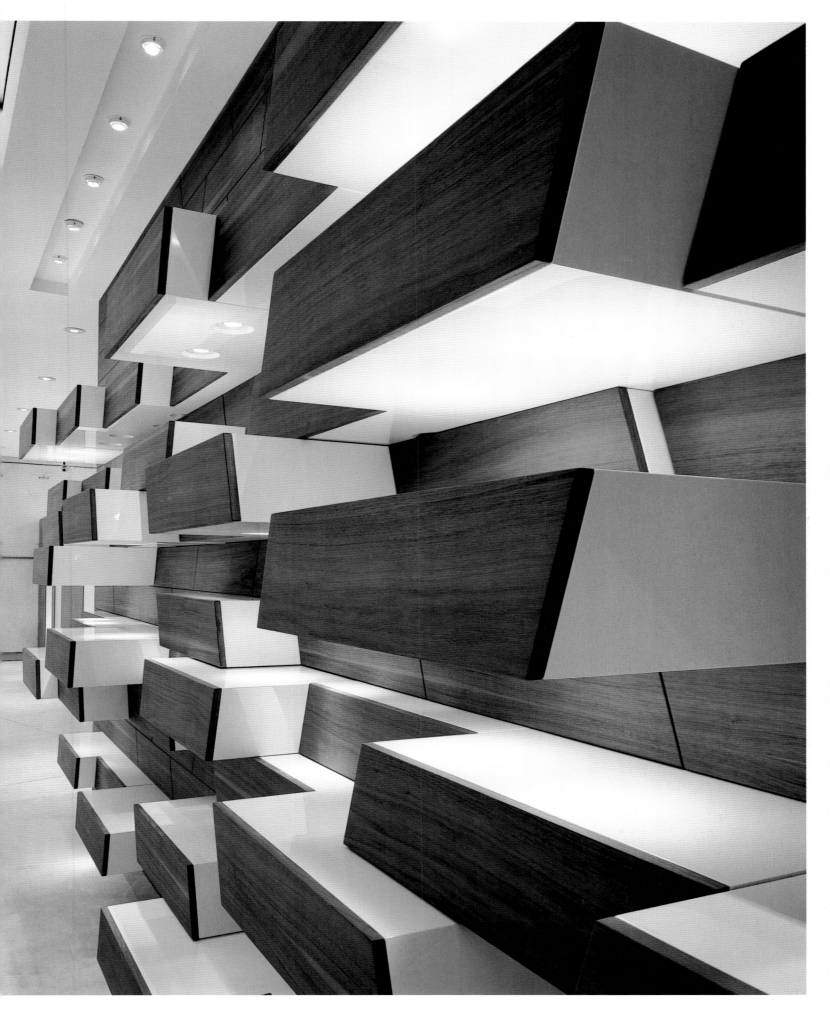

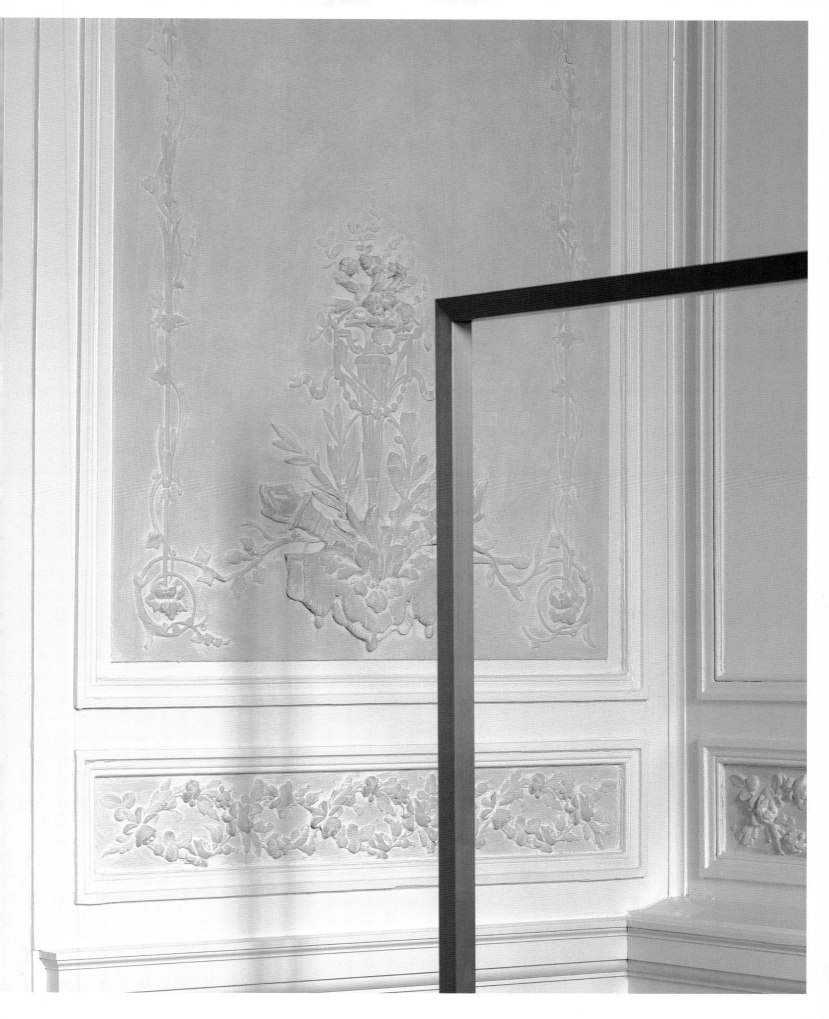

Previous spread: Gabellini Associates, Jil Sander Showroom, Hamburg, 1997. Minimalist steel racks bring the idea of a cabinet to its most reductive form. This spread: Gabellini Associates, Jil Sander Boutique, New York, 2002. Wafer-thin metal shelves recall minimalist sculpture and allow artful display of goods.

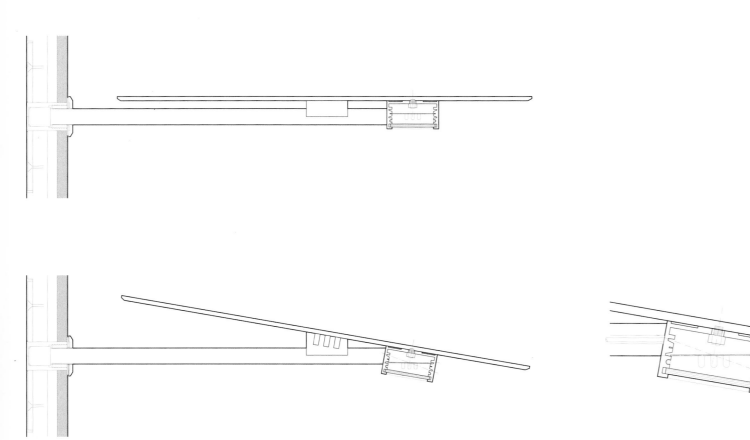

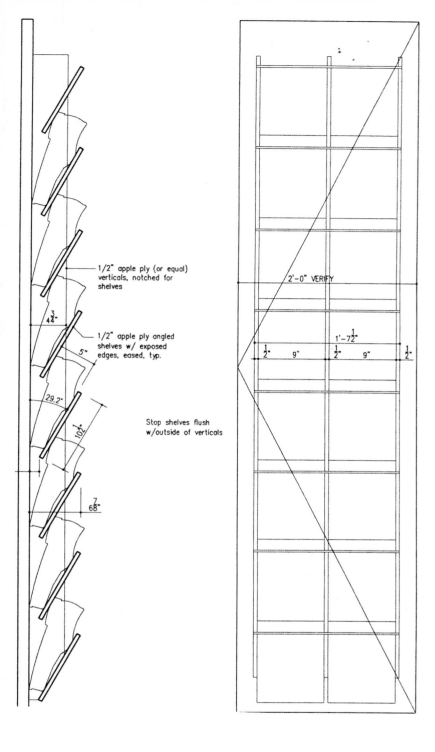

1/2" apple ply (or equal) verticals, notched for shelves

1/2" apple ply angled shelves w/ exposed edges, eased, typ.

Stop shelves flush w/outside of verticals

$4\frac{3}{4}$"

5"

29.2°

10.2°

$\frac{7}{68}$"

2'-0" VERIFY

1'-$7\frac{1}{2}$"

$\frac{1}{2}$" 9" $\frac{1}{2}$" 9" $\frac{1}{2}$"

Eric J. Cobb Architect, Anderson House Addition, Seattle, 2001. A place for everything in which an entire wood wall comprises elegantly fashioned cabinetry offering varied spaces for storage.

Smith and Thompson Architects, Spencer-Booker Loft, NoHo, New York, 1997. A wall, a closet, a window—three disparate elements are combined with a dramatic result.

We are indebted to a large number of people whose help was indispensable in the creation of this book. At Rockport Publishers, our appreciation extends to Ken Fund and Winnie Prentiss for their enormous and unconditional support, the trust they placed in us, and the creative freedoms they allowed. Special thanks are due to Scott Cohen, Doug Dolezal, Eric Höweler, Mimi Moncier, Rob Weiner, and the Chinati Foundation for generously providing images and, in some cases, commentary at various stages of the book's development. To Michael Decker, James McCown, and Lisa Pascarelli, we owe a substantial debt of gratitude for their willingness to be enlisted at the most strenuous moments of editing and production. Rodolfo Machado and Jorge Silvetti provided support without which this project would never have occurred. To Paul Warchol, who opened his extensive photography library to us, we cannot sufficiently express our appreciation or our respect for his work. During several trips to his studio and while sifting through thousands and thousands of images in his archives, we depended upon the kind support of Amy Barkow, Gabrielle Bendiner-Viani, Michele Convery, Bilyana Dimitrova, and Ursula Warchol. And most of all, we are indebted to the creative forces behind the details we have showcased—a list of architects and designers too numerous to recount here. Each deserves our heartfelt thanks.

acknowledgements & dedications

To the memory of GM, who ceaselessly shared her love of words and buildings. —MP

In remembrance of Teresa Testone Pellegrino, whose spirit remains vivid. / En memoria de Teresa Testone Pellegrino, cuyo espíritu permanece vivo.—ORO